MEDITERRANEAN DIET FOR SENIORS OVER 60

A Guide to Healthy Cooking and Eating for Lifelong Wellness – Easy Recipes to Make

Taryn Beckford

Copyright

© 2024 **Taryn Beckford**. All rights reserved. No part of this publication may be reproduced, distributed, or transmitted in any form or by any means, including photocopying, recording, or other electronic or mechanical methods, without the prior written permission of the publisher, except in the case of brief quotations embodied in critical reviews and certain other noncommercial uses permitted by copyright law.

Disclaimer

This book is intended for informational purposes only. It is not a substitute for professional medical advice, diagnosis, or treatment. Always seek the advice of your physician or other qualified health provider with any questions you may have regarding a medical condition or dietary changes. The author and publisher disclaim any liability for any loss or damage arising from the use or misuse of information contained in this book.

CONTENTS

- **INTRODUCTION** 7
- **HEALTHY AGING WITH THE MEDITERRANEAN DIET** 9
  - Understanding the Mediterranean Diet 9
  - Mediterranean Lifestyle Factors 10
  - Why the Mediterranean Diet is Ideal for Seniors 10
  - Adjusting the Mediterranean Diet for Aging Needs 11
  - Getting Started: A Guide to Small Steps 12
  - Essential Mediterranean Pantry Items for Beginners 13
- **BUILDING AN ACCESSIBLE MEDITERRANEAN PANTRY** 15
  - Essential Ingredients in the Mediterranean Diet 15
  - Healthy Fats and Lean Proteins 17
  - Practical Shopping Tips 18
  - Sample Pantry List for Easy Mediterranean Cooking 18
  - Tips for Pantry Organization 19
- **ENERGIZING BREAKFASTS TO START YOUR DAY RIGHT** 21
  - Greek Yogurt Parfait with Berries and Walnuts 22
  - Whole-Grain Avocado Toast with Cherry Tomatoes 23
  - Mediterranean Oatmeal with Almonds and Dried Figs 23
  - Spinach and Feta Omelette 24
  - Fresh Fruit and Ricotta Toast 25
  - Chia Seed Pudding with Fresh Berries 26
  - Shakshuka with Bell Peppers 26
  - Cottage Cheese with Fresh Melon and Mint 27
  - Breakfast Grain Bowl with Quinoa and Soft-Boiled Egg 28
  - Honey-Roasted Nuts and Fruit 29
  - Whole Wheat Pancakes with Fresh Berries 30
  - Mediterranean Breakfast Wrap with Spinach and Hummus 30
  - Savory Oatmeal with Olive Oil and Sundried Tomatoes 31
  - Baked Eggs with Tomatoes and Basil 32
  - Lox and Avocado Bagel with Whole-Grain Bread 32
  - Cottage Cheese and Berry Bowl 33
  - Greek Egg and Spinach Scramble 34
  - Fruit and Nut Breakfast Bowl 34
  - Overnight Oats with Cinnamon and Pear 35
  - Apple Cinnamon Quinoa Porridge 36
  - Greek Yogurt with Pomegranate and Pistachios 37
  - Mediterranean Fruit Salad 37
  - Pita with Labneh and Cucumbers 38
  - Smoothie with Kale, Banana, and Almond Milk 39
  - Banana Walnut Overnight Oats 39
  - Breakfast Bruschetta with Ricotta and Tomatoes 40
  - Egg Muffins with Spinach and Mushrooms 40
  - Tomato and Feta Stuffed Avocado 41
  - Spiced Apple Yogurt Bowl 42
  - Muesli with Fresh Berries and Almonds 43
- **LUNCHES FOR HEART HEALTH AND JOINT SUPPORT** 45

- Key Nutrients and Ingredients for Heart and Joint Health 45
- Recipes (30 Heart-Healthy Lunches) 46
- Mediterranean Chickpea Salad with Lemon-Tahini Dressing 46
- Roasted Red Pepper Hummus Wrap 47
- Greek Lentil Salad with Feta 48
- Roasted Veggie and Quinoa Bowl 49
- Tuna Salad with Olives and Capers 49
- Avocado and Beet Salad 50
- Marinated White Bean and Tomato Salad 51
- Grilled Chicken Salad with Spinach and Olives 51
- Farro and Roasted Vegetable Bowl 52
- Stuffed Pita with Tzatziki and Grilled Veggies 53
- Barley Salad with Roasted Butternut Squash 54
- Mediterranean Cabbage Slaw 55
- Lentil and Spinach Soup 55
- Caprese Salad with Balsamic Reduction 56
- Warm Mediterranean Grain Bowl 57
- Couscous Salad with Feta and Cucumbers 57
- Kale and Cannellini Bean Salad 58
- Panzanella with Cherry Tomatoes and Basil 59
- Spiced Sweet Potato and Chickpea Bowl 60
- Warm Cauliflower and Chickpea Salad 61
- Fennel and Citrus Salad 62
- Grilled Vegetable Sandwich with Pesto 62
- Bulgur Salad with Fresh Herbs 63
- Roasted Beet and Walnut Salad 64
- Mediterranean-Style Tabouleh 64
- Tuna and Cannellini Bean Salad 65
- Spinach and Mushroom Stuffed Bell Peppers 66
- Carrot and Lentil Salad with Lemon Dressing 67
- Roasted Eggplant with Yogurt and Pomegranate 67
- Mediterranean Chickpea and Spinach Stew 68
- Spinach and Mushroom Stuffed Bell Peppers 69
- Carrot and Lentil Salad with Lemon Dressing 69
- Roasted Eggplant with Yogurt and Pomegranate 70
- Mediterranean Chickpea and Spinach Stew 71

DINNERS FOR BONE STRENGTH AND BRAIN HEALTH 73
- Key Nutrients for Bone Strength and Brain Health 73
- Grilled Salmon with Asparagus and Lemon 74
- Baked Chicken with Olives and Artichokes 75
- Ratatouille with Zucchini and Eggplant 76
- Mediterranean Stuffed Peppers 77
- Lemon Herb Shrimp Skewers 77
- Spinach and Feta-Stuffed Chicken 78
- Eggplant Parmesan with Whole-Grain Pasta 79
- Greek Beef Kofta with Tzatziki 79
- Roasted Cod with Olive Tapenade 80
- Lentil and Vegetable Stew 81
- Chicken Souvlaki with Tabbouleh 82
- Pasta Primavera with Fresh Herbs 83
- Chickpea and Spinach Stew 83
- Stuffed Zucchini Boats 84

GRILLED MACKEREL WITH ROASTED VEGETABLES	85
GARLIC SHRIMP WITH COUSCOUS	86
SPAGHETTI SQUASH WITH MARINARA	86
LAMB MEATBALLS WITH YOGURT SAUCE	87
STUFFED EGGPLANT WITH GROUND TURKEY	88
POACHED COD WITH SAFFRON	89
MUSHROOM AND LEEK RISOTTO	90
GREEK-STYLE BAKED FISH	90
CAULIFLOWER AND BROCCOLI STIR-FRY	91
BAKED RATATOUILLE WITH FETA	92
SAUTÉED SWISS CHARD WITH GARLIC AND LEMON	93
ZUCCHINI NOODLES WITH TOMATO BASIL SAUCE	93
MOROCCAN CHICKPEA AND CARROT TAGINE	94
GRILLED LAMB CHOPS WITH ROSEMARY	95
BAKED EGGPLANT WITH MOZZARELLA	95
ARTICHOKE AND SPINACH BAKE	96

NUTRIENT-DENSE SNACKS AND SMALL PLATES ... 99

OLIVE TAPENADE WITH WHOLE-GRAIN CRACKERS	100
GREEK YOGURT DIP WITH CUCUMBER SLICES	101
BAKED ZUCCHINI CHIPS WITH PARMESAN	101
FRESH VEGGIES WITH HUMMUS	102
ROASTED SPICED CHICKPEAS	102
MARINATED OLIVES WITH FETA CUBES	103
DATES STUFFED WITH ALMONDS AND RICOTTA	104
ALMOND BUTTER ON APPLE SLICES	104
CAPRESE SKEWERS WITH CHERRY TOMATOES AND MOZZARELLA	105
WHOLE-WHEAT PITA WITH TZATZIKI	106
STUFFED GRAPE LEAVES	106
CUCUMBER ROUNDS WITH SMOKED SALMON	107
SWEET POTATO TOAST WITH AVOCADO AND TOMATO	108
GREEK YOGURT WITH HONEY AND WALNUTS	108
COTTAGE CHEESE WITH PINEAPPLE AND MINT	109
MINI GREEK SALAD CUPS	109
ALMOND AND FIG ENERGY BITES	110
ROASTED RED PEPPER AND WALNUT DIP	111
SLICED PEARS WITH BLUE CHEESE	111
MEDITERRANEAN BRUSCHETTA WITH OLIVES AND FETA	112
STUFFED BELL PEPPER RINGS WITH HUMMUS	113
BAKED CAULIFLOWER BITES WITH LEMON AND GARLIC	113
FIGS WITH GOAT CHEESE AND WALNUTS	114
AVOCADO DEVILED EGGS	114
ROASTED BEET AND YOGURT DIP	115
SLICED CARROTS WITH GREEK YOGURT RANCH DIP	115
WHOLE-GRAIN CRACKERS WITH LABNEH AND OLIVE OIL	116
CUCUMBER SLICES WITH OLIVE TAPENADE	117
SPINACH AND FETA STUFFED MUSHROOMS	117
MELON AND PROSCIUTTO SKEWERS	118

SATISFYING DESSERTS WITH NATURAL SWEETNESS ... 121

RECIPES (30 NATURALLY SWEETENED DESSERTS)	122
BAKED APPLES WITH CINNAMON AND WALNUTS	122
GREEK YOGURT WITH HONEY AND POMEGRANATE SEEDS	123

- Olive Oil and Lemon Cake 123
- Fresh Fig and Almond Tart 124
- Poached Pears in Red Wine 125
- Ricotta with Fresh Strawberries and Honey 125
- Orange and Almond Flourless Cake 126
- Stuffed Dates with Almonds and Coconut 126
- Lemon Yogurt Parfait with Berries 127
- Watermelon with Feta and Mint 128
- Peach and Honey Skillet Crisp 129
- Frozen Banana Bites with Dark Chocolate 129
- Oat and Almond Cookies 130
- Lemon Ricotta Cheesecake 131
- Baked Pears with Cinnamon and Almonds 131
- Dark Chocolate and Walnut Bark 132
- Berry and Almond Crumble 132
- Sliced Oranges with Pistachios and Honey 133
- Greek-Style Rice Pudding 134
- Coconut Yogurt with Mango and Lime 134
- Baked Figs with Honey and Almonds 135
- Fresh Melon with Prosciutto 136
- Apple and Date Bars 136
- Raspberry Sorbet with Basil 137
- Tahini and Dark Chocolate Cookies 137
- Vanilla Chia Pudding with Berries 138
- Roasted Grapes with Greek Yogurt 139
- Lemon and Olive Oil Biscotti 139
- Fresh Berries with Creamy Ricotta 140
- Dark Chocolate and Date Truffles 141

MEAL PLANNING FOR SENIORS – MAKING IT EASY AND ENJOYABLE 143

- Weekly Meal Plan Samples 144
- Sample Meal Plan for Heart Health 144
- Sample Meal Plan for Inflammation Reduction 145
- Sample Meal Plan for Energy Maintenance 145
- Meal Prep Tips for Efficiency and Enjoyment 146
- Planning for Special Dietary Needs 147
- Preview of Chapter 10: Maintaining a Lifelong Mediterranean Lifestyle 148

30-DAY MEDITERRANEAN MEAL PLAN & TRACKING JOURNAL 149

- 30-Day Meal Plan 149
- Week 1 149
- Week 2 151
- Week 3 152
- Week 4 153
- Wrapping Up: Lifelong Wellness with the Mediterranean Lifestyle 156

INTRODUCTION

Martha, a vibrant 67-year-old, began to notice subtle but undeniable changes in her body. Once an avid walker, she found herself slowing down, feeling more fatigued, and noticing an increased need for medication to manage her blood pressure and cholesterol. Visits to the doctor became frequent reminders of the toll aging could take on her health and lifestyle. But a simple conversation with a friend led her to a life-changing discovery: the Mediterranean diet. As Martha embraced this age-old way of eating, she found herself not only regaining energy but rediscovering the joy of nourishing herself with wholesome, colorful foods. Her weekly meals transformed into an enjoyable ritual, bringing her a newfound vitality and a surprising reduction in her reliance on medications.

For seniors like Martha, nutrition is more than just a choice; it's a pathway to a fulfilling life filled with health, joy, and meaningful connection. As we age, paying attention to our diet becomes crucial in shaping the quality of our golden years. Research shows that adopting the right eating habits can profoundly impact our physical, mental, and emotional well-being. A diet rich in nutrients can support joint health, enhance brain function, reduce inflammation, and lower the risk of chronic conditions such as heart disease and diabetes. And while many diets promise quick fixes, the Mediterranean diet stands apart with its proven, science-backed benefits for seniors. It's not just about choosing a meal plan—it's about investing in a healthful, vibrant future.

The Mediterranean diet isn't new; it's rooted in centuries of tradition. It originated from the countries bordering the Mediterranean Sea, where people naturally embraced a diet filled with fresh vegetables, fruits, lean proteins, whole grains, and heart-healthy fats like olive oil. But this diet is more than the sum of its ingredients; it's a lifestyle that celebrates community, connection, and savoring each meal. Imagine a scene in a small Greek village, where family and friends gather around a table, sharing laughter, stories, and plates of fresh vegetables, grilled fish, and warm bread dipped in rich olive oil. This way of eating nurtures the body and soul, with a deep appreciation for life's simple pleasures and a strong emphasis on sharing these pleasures with loved ones.

In our fast-paced world, it's easy to lose sight of these values. Many seniors face isolation, limited social interaction, and increasing reliance on processed, convenience foods. But the Mediterranean diet brings an invitation to reconnect—not just with wholesome, nourishing food, but with a way of life that values slowing down, savoring each meal, and embracing the company of others. Imagine meals becoming joyful gatherings, whether with family, friends, or community groups, where conversation and laughter are as nourishing as the food on the table.

This book is here to support you in making this powerful transition. Think of the Mediterranean diet not as a restriction or a set of rigid rules but as an empowering choice that invites you to rediscover flavors, textures, and the joy of eating well. With each recipe and chapter, you'll be guided on how to build meals that are nutritious, satisfying, and easy to prepare. Each section is designed to meet the unique needs of seniors, ensuring that you can enjoy every bite while taking care of your body. Whether you're new to the kitchen or a seasoned cook, you'll find that these recipes are accessible and enjoyable.

As you embark on this journey, remember that small steps can create lasting change. Incorporating these Mediterranean principles into your daily life will not only bring health benefits but also the sense of vitality and fulfillment that comes from caring for yourself in the best way possible. Through this book, you are invited to experience the richness, warmth, and healthful benefits of the Mediterranean diet—a lifestyle that celebrates aging gracefully, staying connected, and enjoying life to the fullest.

Welcome to a new chapter of health, happiness, and delicious food. Let's dive in!

HEALTHY AGING WITH THE MEDITERRANEAN DIET

The Mediterranean diet is more than a way of eating—it's a lifestyle that promotes a joyful, balanced, and health-focused approach to life. Rooted in the traditional diets of countries surrounding the Mediterranean Sea, this way of eating has been praised for its health benefits, particularly for seniors. It's not just about the food; it's about nourishing the body, embracing social connections, and enjoying life. For seniors, the Mediterranean diet offers an approach that is as sustainable and enjoyable as it is health-promoting, helping to support heart and brain health, reduce inflammation, and improve energy levels.

Understanding the Mediterranean Diet

The Mediterranean diet is built around nutrient-dense, whole foods and is rich in vegetables, fruits, whole grains, healthy fats, and lean proteins. Each of these components plays a unique role in supporting health, especially as we age.

Origins and Core Principles

At its core, the Mediterranean diet is simple, flexible, and based on traditional foods that people have been eating for centuries:

- **Whole Foods**: The foundation of the Mediterranean diet is whole, unprocessed foods, like fresh vegetables, fruits, legumes, nuts, and whole grains. These foods are packed with essential vitamins, minerals, fiber, and antioxidants—nutrients that are particularly beneficial for seniors as they help support digestion, boost immunity, and reduce the risk of chronic diseases.

- **Healthy Fats**: A cornerstone of the Mediterranean diet is the use of healthy fats, particularly from olive oil, nuts, and fatty fish. Olive oil, rich in monounsaturated fats, helps reduce bad cholesterol and supports heart health. Omega-3 fatty acids from fish like salmon and sardines are linked to improved cognitive health and reduced inflammation, supporting both brain health and joint mobility.

- **Lean Proteins**: The Mediterranean diet focuses on lean sources of protein, including fish, legumes, and poultry. These proteins help maintain muscle mass, which is essential for mobility and balance in seniors. Fish, in particular, is recommended at least twice a week to provide omega-3s, which are crucial for cardiovascular and brain health.

- **Herbs and Spices**: Instead of relying heavily on salt, the Mediterranean diet enhances flavor with herbs and spices like basil, oregano, rosemary, and garlic. This not only reduces sodium intake, supporting heart health, but also boosts antioxidants and anti-inflammatory compounds.

Mediterranean Lifestyle Factors

The Mediterranean diet isn't just about what you eat; it's about how you live. Seniors can benefit from embracing these lifestyle factors to support overall well-being.

- **Social Connections**: Shared meals are a staple of the Mediterranean lifestyle. In countries like Italy and Greece, meals are enjoyed with family and friends, fostering social bonds and reducing feelings of isolation. For seniors, eating with others can enhance emotional well-being and combat loneliness, which is crucial for mental health.

- **Mindful Eating**: Rather than rushing through meals, the Mediterranean approach encourages savoring each bite, focusing on the flavors, and being present during meals. This mindful eating practice can help seniors better recognize hunger cues, improve digestion, and increase satisfaction with smaller portions.

- **Physical Activity**: Gentle daily movement, such as walking, gardening, or stretching, is an integral part of the Mediterranean lifestyle. Physical activity is essential for seniors to maintain strength, balance, and flexibility, which can enhance mobility and reduce the risk of falls.

Why the Mediterranean Diet is Ideal for Seniors

The Mediterranean diet is uniquely suited to meet the needs of seniors, helping them maintain a healthy weight, support heart and brain health, and improve quality of life. Here's how it addresses common health concerns for aging adults:

1. Heart Health

Heart disease remains a leading concern for seniors. The Mediterranean diet, rich in fruits, vegetables, whole grains, and healthy fats, has been shown to lower cholesterol and reduce high blood pressure. Olive oil, nuts, and fatty fish work together to support cardiovascular health, lowering the risk of heart attacks and strokes.

2. Brain Health and Cognitive Support

Cognitive decline is a common concern as we age. Fortunately, the Mediterranean diet is rich in nutrients that protect against dementia and memory loss. Omega-3 fatty acids from fish, along with antioxidants from fruits and vegetables, help reduce inflammation and oxidative stress, supporting long-term brain health and cognitive function.

3. Reduced Inflammation and Improved Mobility

Arthritis and joint pain can limit mobility and affect quality of life. The Mediterranean diet is naturally anti-inflammatory due to its focus on plant-based foods, healthy fats, and lean proteins. Foods like olive oil, nuts, and leafy greens help reduce inflammation, potentially alleviating symptoms of arthritis and improving joint function.

4. Better Digestive Health

As we age, digestive issues like constipation can become more common. The Mediterranean diet includes fiber-rich foods, such as whole grains, fruits, and vegetables, that support gut health, aid in regular digestion, and promote a healthy microbiome.

5. Energy and Vitality

The Mediterranean diet provides a balanced mix of macronutrients—healthy fats, lean proteins, and complex carbohydrates—that give seniors sustained energy throughout the day. The diet's emphasis on natural, unprocessed foods ensures that energy levels remain steady, which is especially important for seniors who may experience fatigue or sluggishness.

Adjusting the Mediterranean Diet for Aging Needs

As seniors have unique nutritional requirements, it's important to adapt the Mediterranean diet to ensure it meets these needs:

Key Nutrients for Seniors

- **Calcium and Vitamin D**: Bone density decreases with age, which can lead to osteoporosis. It's essential to incorporate foods rich in calcium (such as leafy greens, dairy products, and sardines) and vitamin D (found in fortified foods and fatty fish) to support bone health.

- **Fiber**: Fiber helps maintain digestive health, regulates blood sugar levels, and supports heart health. Seniors should include fiber-rich foods like oats, legumes, fruits, and vegetables in their daily diet.

- **Lean Protein**: Muscle mass tends to decline with age, which can impact mobility and strength. Seniors should aim for lean proteins such as fish, eggs, and poultry, which are staples in the Mediterranean diet and help maintain muscle health.

Addressing Common Aging-Related Issues

- **Reduced Appetite**: Some seniors may struggle with decreased appetite. The Mediterranean diet offers nutrient-dense options that provide ample calories in small portions. Healthy fats from olive oil, avocados, and nuts are ideal for adding calories without needing to increase portion sizes significantly.

- **Digestive Sensitivities**: Foods that are harder to digest may need to be limited. Seniors can prioritize cooked vegetables, soft fruits, and whole grains that are easy on the stomach. Pureeing or mashing certain foods, like legumes, can make them easier to digest.

- **Nutrient Absorption**: Nutrient absorption may decrease with age, particularly for vitamin B12 and iron. Seniors can enhance their intake by incorporating fortified foods and, if necessary, considering supplements with guidance from a healthcare provider.

Getting Started: A Guide to Small Steps

Transitioning to the Mediterranean diet doesn't need to be overwhelming. Here are some small, practical steps for seniors to gradually adopt this diet:

Simple Steps to Start Eating Mediterranean

1. **Begin with One Meal per Day**: Start by making one meal Mediterranean each day, such as breakfast. A simple option could be Greek yogurt with fresh berries and a sprinkle of nuts, or whole-grain toast with avocado and a boiled egg.

2. **Add Vegetables to Every Meal**: Incorporate at least one serving of vegetables with each meal. Add spinach to your morning omelet, enjoy a side salad with lunch, or include roasted vegetables with dinner. This small habit can have a big impact on overall nutrition.

3. **Use Olive Oil Instead of Butter**: When cooking or dressing salads, opt for olive oil. It's a healthier fat that enhances the flavors of Mediterranean foods and supports heart health.

4. **Opt for Whole Grains**: Choose whole grains like brown rice, quinoa, and whole-wheat bread over refined grains. These grains are high in fiber, which supports digestive health and helps regulate blood sugar.

5. **Incorporate Fish Twice a Week**: Make a habit of including fish in your diet at least twice a week. Fish like salmon, sardines, and trout are rich in omega-3 fatty acids, which are essential for heart and brain health.

Essential Mediterranean Pantry Items for Beginners

Building a Mediterranean-friendly pantry makes it easier to create nutritious meals. Here are some essential items to keep on hand:

- **Olive Oil**: Use it as the primary cooking oil for its heart-healthy fats.
- **Whole Grains**: Stock up on options like quinoa, whole-wheat pasta, brown rice, and oats.
- **Legumes**: Chickpeas, lentils, and black beans are versatile and provide plant-based protein.
- **Nuts and Seeds**: Almonds, walnuts, chia seeds, and sunflower seeds are great for snacks or adding to meals.
- **Herbs and Spices**: Oregano, basil, rosemary, garlic, and thyme add flavor without extra salt.
- **Fresh and Dried Fruits**: Berries, apples, figs, and dates provide natural sweetness and antioxidants.
- **Leafy Greens**: Keep spinach, kale, and other greens for salads, soups, and side dishes.
- **Fish and Lean Proteins**: Frozen or canned fish, like tuna and salmon, and lean poultry are convenient options.

Preview of Chapter 2: Building an Accessible Mediterranean Pantry

In Chapter 2, we'll explore how to stock your pantry for Mediterranean cooking with ease, including tips for sourcing ingredients, budget-friendly shopping strategies, and pantry organization. This chapter will guide seniors in creating a kitchen that supports health-focused eating and ensures that every meal is just a few ingredients away.

BUILDING AN ACCESSIBLE MEDITERRANEAN PANTRY

A well-stocked pantry is the foundation of any diet, and for seniors adopting the Mediterranean lifestyle, having the right ingredients on hand can make cooking more convenient, enjoyable, and affordable. By organizing a pantry with staple ingredients, seniors can ensure they have nutritious options ready to go, reducing stress around meal prep and empowering them to cook meals that are both health-promoting and delicious.

Essential Ingredients in the Mediterranean Diet

The Mediterranean pantry emphasizes whole, nutrient-dense foods that are versatile and flavorful. These ingredients—such as olive oil, whole grains, legumes, nuts, and fresh or dried herbs—are packed with vitamins, minerals, fiber, and healthy fats that support heart, brain, and digestive health.

Olive Oil

Olive oil is a cornerstone of the Mediterranean diet and is often used in cooking, baking, and dressing salads. It's high in monounsaturated fats, which help improve cholesterol levels, reduce inflammation, and promote heart health.

- **Types of Olive Oil**: Extra virgin olive oil (EVOO) is less processed and has a stronger flavor and more antioxidants than regular olive oil, making it ideal for salad dressings and dips. Regular olive oil is better for cooking at higher temperatures.

- **Storage Tip**: Store olive oil in a cool, dark place and use within a few months of opening to preserve its flavor and nutrients.

Whole Grains

Whole grains provide essential fiber, complex carbohydrates, and minerals. They help regulate blood sugar, support digestion, and sustain energy levels. Examples include quinoa, brown rice, oats, farro, and whole-wheat pasta.

- **How to Use**: Whole grains are versatile and can be used as a base for salads, side dishes, or breakfasts. For example, cook a batch of quinoa or brown rice at the start of the week to add to salads or use as a side.
- **Quick Options**: Quick-cook oats, pre-cooked rice, and whole-grain pasta are excellent pantry additions for busy days.

Seasonal Fruits and Vegetables

Fresh fruits and vegetables are vital to the Mediterranean diet, providing vitamins, fiber, and antioxidants. Eating seasonally is beneficial for budget and flavor, as produce tends to be less expensive and more flavorful when in season.

- **Common Mediterranean Vegetables**: Tomatoes, zucchini, cucumbers, bell peppers, spinach, and leafy greens.
- **Common Mediterranean Fruits**: Apples, oranges, figs, grapes, and berries.
- **Tip for Seniors**: Frozen fruits and vegetables are excellent alternatives when fresh produce isn't available. They're easy to store, retain most of their nutrients, and can be used in smoothies, soups, and stews.

Legumes

Legumes, including lentils, chickpeas, and beans, are rich in fiber, plant-based protein, and essential nutrients like magnesium and potassium. They're heart-healthy, support digestion, and help stabilize blood sugar levels.

- **Convenience Tip**: Canned legumes are convenient and cost-effective. Rinse them before use to reduce sodium, or opt for low-sodium varieties.
- **Uses**: Legumes can be added to salads, soups, and stews or blended into spreads like hummus for a nutrient-dense snack.

Nuts and Seeds

Nuts and seeds, such as almonds, walnuts, chia seeds, and pumpkin seeds, offer healthy fats, fiber, and protein. They're easy to add to meals and make excellent snacks, promoting heart health and sustained energy.

- **Tip**: Buy unsalted nuts to avoid excess sodium, and store them in the fridge or freezer to extend freshness.
- **Quick Use**: Sprinkle nuts and seeds over salads, yogurt, or oatmeal for extra crunch and nutrients.

Herbs and Spices

Herbs and spices are essential for adding flavor to Mediterranean dishes without excess salt. They are rich in antioxidants and anti-inflammatory compounds, enhancing both the flavor and health benefits of meals.

- **Common Herbs and Spices**: Basil, oregano, rosemary, thyme, cinnamon, turmeric, and garlic.
- **Tip**: Invest in both dried and fresh herbs if possible. Growing your own fresh herbs can be a fun, cost-effective way to enhance your meals. Basil, rosemary, and thyme are easy to grow indoors.

Healthy Fats and Lean Proteins

The Mediterranean diet is abundant in heart-healthy fats and lean protein sources that support heart health, cognitive function, and muscle maintenance, which are essential for aging well.

Heart-Healthy Fats

Heart-healthy fats are found in foods like olive oil, avocados, and nuts. These fats improve cholesterol levels, provide energy, and reduce inflammation.

- **Olive Oil**: Use as the primary cooking oil for sautés, salad dressings, and dipping.
- **Nuts and Seeds**: Incorporate almonds, walnuts, chia seeds, and flaxseeds into meals and snacks.
- **Avocados**: Avocados are nutrient-dense and versatile. Enjoy them on toast, in salads, or blended into dips.

Lean Proteins

Protein is crucial for muscle maintenance and immune function. The Mediterranean diet emphasizes fish, legumes, and moderate amounts of poultry and eggs, rather than red meat.

- **Fish**: Fatty fish like salmon, sardines, and mackerel are excellent sources of omega-3 fatty acids, which are linked to heart and brain health. Aim to have fish twice a week.
- **Legumes**: Chickpeas, lentils, and beans provide plant-based protein, fiber, and minerals.
- **Poultry and Eggs**: Chicken, turkey, and eggs are good sources of lean protein and easy to incorporate into a variety of dishes.
- **Tip**: Choose wild-caught fish and organic poultry whenever possible to reduce exposure to additives and support environmental sustainability.

Practical Shopping Tips

Shopping smartly is key to maintaining a Mediterranean pantry on a budget. By following these tips, seniors can stock up on high-quality, nutritious ingredients without overspending.

Grocery Shopping for Seasonal and Budget-Friendly Ingredients

- **Choose Seasonal Produce**: Seasonal produce is fresher, tastier, and usually more affordable. Check local farmers' markets or grocery stores for what's in season.
- **Bulk Buy Grains and Legumes**: Whole grains and legumes like rice, oats, and beans can be bought in bulk, reducing cost and ensuring you have staples on hand.
- **Frozen and Canned Options**: Frozen fruits and vegetables retain most of their nutrients and are convenient when fresh produce isn't available. Canned options, like tomatoes and legumes, are budget-friendly and versatile.

Senior-Friendly Shopping Tips

- **Online Shopping and Delivery Services**: Many stores offer delivery or curbside pickup, which can be convenient for seniors with mobility issues.
- **Create a Grocery List**: Keeping a list of staples and meal essentials helps prevent impulse buys and ensures you always have the ingredients you need.
- **Plan for Leftovers**: Buy ingredients that can be used across several meals. For example, roasted vegetables can be used in salads, wraps, or as sides, making meal prep easier and more economical.

Sample Pantry List for Easy Mediterranean Cooking

This list includes essential Mediterranean ingredients that are affordable, nutritious, and versatile, making it easy for seniors to create balanced meals.

Core Pantry Staples

- **Olive Oil**: Extra virgin for salads and dipping; regular for cooking.
- **Whole Grains**: Quinoa, brown rice, oats, farro, and whole-wheat pasta.
- **Legumes**: Canned or dried chickpeas, lentils, and black beans.
- **Nuts and Seeds**: Almonds, walnuts, chia seeds, and pumpkin seeds.
- **Herbs and Spices**: Basil, oregano, rosemary, thyme, cinnamon, and garlic.
- **Vinegar**: Balsamic, red wine, or apple cider vinegar for dressings and marinades.
- **Garlic and Onions**: Fresh garlic and onions enhance flavor in most Mediterranean dishes.

Fresh and Frozen Items

- **Vegetables**: Tomatoes, cucumbers, bell peppers, spinach, kale, zucchini, and eggplant.
- **Fruits**: Apples, oranges, lemons, figs, and berries.
- **Fish**: Frozen or canned salmon, sardines, and tuna.
- **Lean Proteins**: Eggs, chicken breast, and turkey.
- **Avocados**: For salads, spreads, and sides.

Example Pantry-Based Recipes

Here are some simple recipe ideas using these pantry items:

1. **Mediterranean Chickpea Salad**: Canned chickpeas, cucumbers, tomatoes, onions, fresh parsley, olive oil, and lemon juice.
2. **Simple Grain Bowl**: Quinoa or brown rice, sautéed vegetables, a boiled egg, and a drizzle of olive oil.
3. **Overnight Oats with Fruit and Nuts**: Oats, milk (or milk alternative), berries, and a handful of nuts.

Tips for Pantry Organization

A well-organized pantry makes cooking simpler and ensures you can quickly find what you need:

- **Use Clear Containers**: Store grains, nuts, and legumes in clear, labeled containers to keep them fresh and easy to locate.
- **Prioritize High-Use Items**: Keep olive oil, grains, and canned goods within easy reach.
- **Rotate Stock**: When you restock, place newer items behind older ones to ensure you use ingredients before they expire.

With this Mediterranean pantry, seniors will have the essential tools to prepare balanced, nutritious meals that support their health goals. By selecting versatile, high-quality ingredients and organizing their pantry effectively, they can enjoy convenient, budget-friendly meals that align with the Mediterranean lifestyle.

Preview of Chapter 3: Energizing Breakfasts to Start Your Day Right

In Chapter 3, we'll explore breakfast recipes designed to boost energy and mental clarity. From protein-packed Greek yogurt parfaits to savory vegetable omelets, these breakfasts offer nutrient-rich options that support senior health and provide a delicious start to each day.

ENERGIZING BREAKFASTS TO START YOUR DAY RIGHT

Breakfast plays a vital role in supporting energy, cognitive function, and digestive ease throughout the day. For seniors, a balanced breakfast can help regulate blood sugar, improve focus, and boost overall vitality. Breakfast is also an opportunity to incorporate nutrient-dense foods that provide essential fiber, healthy fats, and protein, which help stabilize energy levels and reduce cravings later in the day.

Key Benefits of a Balanced Breakfast

- **Blood Sugar Regulation**: Including complex carbohydrates and fiber in breakfast slows digestion, preventing spikes and crashes in blood sugar levels, which helps maintain stable energy throughout the day.

- **Brain Health**: A morning meal rich in antioxidants, healthy fats, and protein can support cognitive function, memory, and mental clarity, which are especially important for seniors.

- **Digestive Ease**: Fiber-rich foods such as whole grains, fruits, and vegetables support digestive health, promoting regularity and reducing the risk of constipation.

Recipes (30 Energizing Breakfasts)

Below are 30 Mediterranean-inspired breakfast recipes that are both flavorful and nutritious. Each recipe includes ingredients, detailed steps, preparation time, servings, and nutritional information per serving.

Greek Yogurt Parfait with Berries and Walnuts

Ingredients:

- 1 cup Greek yogurt
- 1/2 cup mixed berries (blueberries, strawberries, raspberries)
- 2 tbsp chopped walnuts
- 1 tsp honey (optional)

Preparation:

1. In a bowl or glass, layer half the Greek yogurt.
2. Add a layer of berries and walnuts.
3. Repeat layers, topping with a drizzle of honey, if desired.

Time to Prepare: 5 minutes

Servings: 1

Nutritional Value per Serving:
- Calories: 180
- Protein: 12g
- Fiber: 4g
- Healthy Fats: 8g

Whole-Grain Avocado Toast with Cherry Tomatoes

Ingredients:
- 1 slice whole-grain bread
- 1/2 avocado, mashed
- 5-6 cherry tomatoes, halved
- Salt and pepper, to taste
- Fresh basil, for garnish (optional)

Preparation:
1. Toast the whole-grain bread until golden.
2. Spread mashed avocado over the toast.
3. Top with cherry tomatoes and sprinkle with salt, pepper, and basil.

Time to Prepare: 5 minutes

Servings: 1

Nutritional Value per Serving:
- Calories: 220
- Protein: 6g
- Fiber: 7g
- Healthy Fats: 12g

Mediterranean Oatmeal with Almonds and Dried Figs

Ingredients:
- 1/2 cup oats
- 1 cup water or milk of choice
- 1 tbsp sliced almonds
- 2 dried figs, chopped
- 1/2 tsp cinnamon

Preparation:
1. In a small pot, bring water or milk to a boil and add oats.
2. Reduce heat and simmer for 5-7 minutes, stirring occasionally.
3. Once oats are tender, stir in cinnamon.
4. Top with almonds and figs before serving.

Time to Prepare: 10 minutes

Servings: 1

Nutritional Value per Serving:
- Calories: 280
- Protein: 8g
- Fiber: 6g
- Healthy Fats: 6g

Spinach and Feta Omelette

Ingredients:
- 2 large eggs
- 1/4 cup fresh spinach, chopped
- 1 tbsp crumbled feta cheese
- Salt and pepper, to taste
- 1 tsp olive oil

Preparation:
1. In a bowl, whisk the eggs with salt and pepper.
2. Heat olive oil in a non-stick pan over medium heat.

3. Add spinach and cook until wilted.
4. Pour eggs over spinach and cook until set, then sprinkle with feta.
5. Fold the omelette and serve warm.

Time to Prepare: 10 minutes

Servings: 1

Nutritional Value per Serving:
- Calories: 200
- Protein: 14g
- Fiber: 1g
- Healthy Fats: 14g

Fresh Fruit and Ricotta Toast

Ingredients:
- 1 slice whole-grain bread
- 1/4 cup ricotta cheese
- 1/2 apple or pear, thinly sliced
- 1 tsp honey
- A pinch of cinnamon

Preparation:
1. Toast the whole-grain bread.
2. Spread ricotta cheese on toast.
3. Layer with fruit slices, drizzle honey, and sprinkle cinnamon.

Time to Prepare: 5 minutes

Servings: 1

Nutritional Value per Serving:
- Calories: 210
- Protein: 10g
- Fiber: 4g
- Healthy Fats: 8g

Chia Seed Pudding with Fresh Berries

Ingredients:

- 3 tbsp chia seeds
- 1 cup almond milk (or milk of choice)
- 1/2 cup mixed berries
- 1 tsp honey (optional)

Preparation:

1. In a bowl, mix chia seeds and almond milk.
2. Stir well and refrigerate for 1-2 hours or overnight until thickened.
3. Top with fresh berries and a drizzle of honey before serving.

Time to Prepare: 5 minutes (plus chilling time)

Servings: 1

Nutritional Value per Serving:

- Calories: 150
- Protein: 5g
- Fiber: 8g
- Healthy Fats: 7g

Shakshuka with Bell Peppers

Ingredients:

- 1/2 tbsp olive oil
- 1/4 onion, diced
- 1/2 bell pepper, diced
- 1/2 cup crushed tomatoes
- 1 large egg
- Salt and pepper, to taste
- Fresh parsley, for garnish

Preparation:

1. Heat olive oil in a pan over medium heat. Sauté onions and bell peppers until softened.
2. Add crushed tomatoes, salt, and pepper. Simmer for 5 minutes.

3. Make a well in the sauce and crack the egg into it.
4. Cover and cook until the egg is set to your liking.
5. Garnish with parsley and serve with whole-grain bread.

Time to Prepare: 15 minutes

Servings: 1

Nutritional Value per Serving:
- Calories: 160
- Protein: 7g
- Fiber: 3g
- Healthy Fats: 6g

Cottage Cheese with Fresh Melon and Mint

Ingredients:
- 1 cup cottage cheese
- 1/2 cup cubed melon (cantaloupe or honeydew)
- Fresh mint leaves, chopped
- 1 tsp honey (optional)

Preparation:
1. Place cottage cheese in a bowl.
2. Top with cubed melon and sprinkle with mint.
3. Drizzle honey on top if desired.

Time to Prepare: 5 minutes

Servings: 1

Nutritional Value per Serving:
- Calories: 180
- Protein: 14g
- Fiber: 1g
- Healthy Fats: 2g

Breakfast Grain Bowl with Quinoa and Soft-Boiled Egg

Ingredients:

- 1/2 cup cooked quinoa
- 1 large egg
- 1/4 avocado, sliced
- 1 tbsp crumbled feta cheese
- Salt and pepper, to taste

Preparation:

1. Bring a small pot of water to a boil and add the egg. Cook for 6 minutes, then transfer to cold water to cool.
2. In a bowl, layer the cooked quinoa, sliced avocado, and crumbled feta.
3. Peel the egg, cut it in half, and place on top of the bowl.
4. Season with salt and pepper before serving.

Time to Prepare: 10 minutes

Servings: 1

Nutritional Value per Serving:

- Calories: 250
- Protein: 12g
- Fiber: 6g
- Healthy Fats: 10g

Honey-Roasted Nuts and Fruit

Ingredients:

- 1/4 cup mixed nuts (almonds, walnuts, and pecans)
- 1 tsp honey
- 1/2 cup fresh berries

Preparation:

1. Preheat the oven to 350°F (175°C).
2. Toss nuts with honey and spread on a baking sheet.
3. Roast for 5-7 minutes, until golden.
4. Let cool, then serve with fresh berries.

Time to Prepare: 10 minutes

Servings: 1

Nutritional Value per Serving:

- Calories: 200
- Protein: 5g
- Fiber: 4g

- Healthy Fats: 12g

Whole Wheat Pancakes with Fresh Berries

Ingredients:

- 1/2 cup whole wheat flour
- 1/2 tsp baking powder
- 1/2 cup milk (or milk alternative)
- 1 egg
- 1/4 cup fresh berries (blueberries, strawberries)

Preparation:

1. Mix flour and baking powder in a bowl.
2. In another bowl, whisk the egg and milk.
3. Combine wet and dry ingredients and stir until smooth.
4. Heat a non-stick skillet and pour in 1/4 cup batter.
5. Cook until bubbles form, then flip. Serve with fresh berries.

Time to Prepare: 15 minutes

Servings: 2

Nutritional Value per Serving:

- Calories: 150
- Protein: 6g
- Fiber: 3g
- Healthy Fats: 4g

Mediterranean Breakfast Wrap with Spinach and Hummus

Ingredients:

- 1 whole-wheat tortilla
- 2 tbsp hummus
- 1/4 cup fresh spinach leaves

- 1/4 cup cucumber, sliced
- 1 tbsp crumbled feta cheese

Preparation:
1. Spread hummus evenly over the tortilla.
2. Layer spinach, cucumber, and feta cheese on one half.
3. Roll the tortilla tightly and cut in half to serve.

Time to Prepare: 5 minutes

Servings: 1

Nutritional Value per Serving:
- Calories: 220
- Protein: 8g
- Fiber: 5g
- Healthy Fats: 10g

Savory Oatmeal with Olive Oil and Sundried Tomatoes

Ingredients:
- 1/2 cup oats
- 1 cup water or milk
- 1 tbsp chopped sundried tomatoes
- 1 tsp olive oil
- Salt and pepper, to taste

Preparation:
1. Bring water or milk to a boil, add oats, and reduce heat to simmer.
2. Cook for 5-7 minutes, stirring occasionally.
3. Stir in sundried tomatoes, olive oil, salt, and pepper.
4. Serve warm.

Time to Prepare: 10 minutes

Servings: 1

Nutritional Value per Serving:

- Calories: 210
- Protein: 6g
- Fiber: 5g
- Healthy Fats: 8g

Baked Eggs with Tomatoes and Basil

Ingredients:
- 1/2 cup cherry tomatoes, halved
- 2 large eggs
- Salt and pepper, to taste
- Fresh basil, chopped

Preparation:
1. Preheat the oven to 375°F (190°C).
2. Place tomatoes in a small baking dish.
3. Crack eggs over tomatoes and season with salt and pepper.
4. Bake for 10-12 minutes, until whites are set.
5. Garnish with fresh basil before serving.

Time to Prepare: 15 minutes

Servings: 1

Nutritional Value per Serving:
- Calories: 180
- Protein: 12g
- Fiber: 2g
- Healthy Fats: 8g

Lox and Avocado Bagel with Whole-Grain Bread

Ingredients:
- 1 whole-grain bagel
- 1/4 avocado, mashed

- 1 oz smoked salmon
- Fresh dill, for garnish

Preparation:

1. Toast the bagel halves until golden.
2. Spread mashed avocado over each half.
3. Top with smoked salmon and garnish with dill.

Time to Prepare: 5 minutes

Servings: 1

Nutritional Value per Serving:

- Calories: 280
- Protein: 14g
- Fiber: 6g
- Healthy Fats: 12g

Cottage Cheese and Berry Bowl

Ingredients:

- 1 cup cottage cheese
- 1/2 cup mixed berries
- 1 tbsp slivered almonds

Preparation:

1. Place cottage cheese in a bowl.
2. Top with berries and almonds.
3. Serve immediately.

Time to Prepare: 5 minutes

Servings: 1

Nutritional Value per Serving:

- Calories: 210
- Protein: 14g
- Fiber: 3g
- Healthy Fats: 7g

Greek Egg and Spinach Scramble

Ingredients:

- 2 large eggs
- 1/4 cup fresh spinach, chopped
- 1 tbsp crumbled feta cheese
- Salt and pepper, to taste
- 1 tsp olive oil

Preparation:

1. In a bowl, whisk the eggs with salt and pepper.
2. Heat olive oil in a non-stick skillet over medium heat.
3. Add spinach and cook until wilted, about 1 minute.
4. Pour in the eggs and scramble until fully cooked.
5. Sprinkle with feta cheese before serving.

Time to Prepare: 10 minutes

Servings: 1

Nutritional Value per Serving:

- Calories: 180
- Protein: 12g
- Fiber: 1g
- Healthy Fats: 12g

Fruit and Nut Breakfast Bowl

Ingredients:

- 1/2 cup Greek yogurt
- 1/4 cup mixed fresh fruits (apple, pear, or berries)
- 1 tbsp chopped walnuts
- 1 tsp honey

Preparation:

1. Place Greek yogurt in a bowl.

2. Top with fresh fruits and walnuts.
3. Drizzle with honey.

Time to Prepare: 5 minutes

Servings: 1

Nutritional Value per Serving:
- Calories: 180
- Protein: 10g
- Fiber: 3g
- Healthy Fats: 7g

Overnight Oats with Cinnamon and Pear

Ingredients:
- 1/2 cup rolled oats
- 1/2 cup milk or almond milk
- 1/2 pear, diced
- 1/4 tsp cinnamon
- 1 tsp chia seeds

Preparation:
1. In a jar, combine oats, milk, pear, cinnamon, and chia seeds.
2. Stir well, cover, and refrigerate overnight.
3. Serve cold or warm.

Time to Prepare: 5 minutes (plus overnight refrigeration)

Servings: 1

Nutritional Value per Serving:
- Calories: 200
- Protein: 6g
- Fiber: 6g
- Healthy Fats: 4g

Apple Cinnamon Quinoa Porridge

Ingredients:

- 1/2 cup cooked quinoa
- 1/2 cup milk or almond milk
- 1/4 apple, diced
- 1/4 tsp cinnamon
- 1 tsp honey

Preparation:

1. In a saucepan, combine quinoa, milk, and diced apple.
2. Heat over medium heat until warm, stirring occasionally.
3. Stir in cinnamon and honey before serving.

Time to Prepare: 10 minutes

Servings: 1

Nutritional Value per Serving:

- Calories: 190
- Protein: 6g

- Fiber: 4g
- Healthy Fats: 3g

Greek Yogurt with Pomegranate and Pistachios

Ingredients:
- 1 cup Greek yogurt
- 2 tbsp pomegranate seeds
- 1 tbsp chopped pistachios
- 1 tsp honey

Preparation:
1. Place Greek yogurt in a bowl.
2. Top with pomegranate seeds and pistachios.
3. Drizzle honey on top before serving.

Time to Prepare: 5 minutes

Servings: 1

Nutritional Value per Serving:
- Calories: 220
- Protein: 14g
- Fiber: 3g
- Healthy Fats: 8g

Mediterranean Fruit Salad

Ingredients:
- 1/2 cup diced watermelon
- 1/2 cup diced cantaloupe
- 1/4 cup grapes, halved
- Fresh mint leaves, chopped
- 1 tsp lemon juice

Preparation:

1. In a bowl, combine watermelon, cantaloupe, and grapes.
2. Sprinkle with chopped mint and drizzle lemon juice on top.
3. Toss to combine and serve fresh.

Time to Prepare: 5 minutes

Servings: 1

Nutritional Value per Serving:

- Calories: 80
- Protein: 1g
- Fiber: 2g
- Healthy Fats: 0g

Pita with Labneh and Cucumbers

Ingredients:

- 1 small whole-grain pita
- 2 tbsp labneh (strained yogurt)
- 1/4 cup cucumber slices
- Fresh dill, for garnish

Preparation:

1. Spread labneh over the pita.
2. Arrange cucumber slices on top.
3. Garnish with fresh dill and serve.

Time to Prepare: 5 minutes

Servings: 1

Nutritional Value per Serving:

- Calories: 150
- Protein: 6g
- Fiber: 3g
- Healthy Fats: 5g

Smoothie with Kale, Banana, and Almond Milk

Ingredients:

- 1 cup kale leaves, chopped
- 1/2 banana
- 1 cup almond milk
- 1 tsp honey (optional)

Preparation:

1. In a blender, combine kale, banana, and almond milk.
2. Blend until smooth, adding honey if desired.
3. Serve immediately.

Time to Prepare: 5 minutes

Servings: 1

Nutritional Value per Serving:

- Calories: 120
- Protein: 3g
- Fiber: 3g
- Healthy Fats: 2g

Banana Walnut Overnight Oats

Ingredients:

- 1/2 cup rolled oats
- 1/2 cup milk or almond milk
- 1/2 banana, sliced
- 1 tbsp chopped walnuts
- 1/4 tsp cinnamon

Preparation:

1. In a jar, combine oats, milk, banana, walnuts, and cinnamon.
2. Stir well, cover, and refrigerate overnight.
3. Serve cold or warm.

Time to Prepare: 5 minutes (plus overnight refrigeration)

Servings: 1

Nutritional Value per Serving:
- Calories: 220
- Protein: 6g
- Fiber: 5g
- Healthy Fats: 6g

Breakfast Bruschetta with Ricotta and Tomatoes

Ingredients:
- 1 slice whole-grain bread
- 2 tbsp ricotta cheese
- 3 cherry tomatoes, halved
- Fresh basil, for garnish

Preparation:
1. Toast the whole-grain bread until golden.
2. Spread ricotta on the toast.
3. Top with cherry tomatoes and garnish with basil.

Time to Prepare: 5 minutes

Servings: 1

Nutritional Value per Serving:
- Calories: 170
- Protein: 8g
- Fiber: 3g
- Healthy Fats: 5g

Egg Muffins with Spinach and Mushrooms

Ingredients:
- 4 large eggs
- 1/4 cup chopped spinach

- 1/4 cup diced mushrooms
- Salt and pepper, to taste
- 1 tsp olive oil

Preparation:

1. Preheat oven to 350°F (175°C) and grease a muffin tin.
2. In a bowl, whisk eggs with salt and pepper.
3. Stir in spinach and mushrooms.
4. Pour mixture into muffin tin and bake for 15-18 minutes until set.

Time to Prepare: 20 minutes

Servings: 2

Nutritional Value per Serving:

- Calories: 110
- Protein: 8g
- Fiber: 1g
- Healthy Fats: 7g

Tomato and Feta Stuffed Avocado

Ingredients:

- 1/2 avocado
- 2 cherry tomatoes, diced
- 1 tbsp crumbled feta cheese
- Fresh basil, chopped

Preparation:

1. Scoop a small amount of flesh from the avocado half to make room for filling.
2. In a bowl, combine diced tomatoes, feta, and basil.
3. Spoon mixture into the avocado half and serve.

Time to Prepare: 5 minutes

Servings: 1

Nutritional Value per Serving:

- Calories: 160

- Protein: 4g
- Fiber: 6g
- Healthy Fats: 12g

Spiced Apple Yogurt Bowl

Ingredients:
- 1/2 cup Greek yogurt
- 1/4 apple, diced
- 1/4 tsp cinnamon
- 1 tsp honey
- 1 tbsp chopped walnuts

Preparation:
1. Place Greek yogurt in a bowl.
2. Top with diced apple, sprinkle cinnamon, and drizzle with honey.
3. Add walnuts and serve.

Time to Prepare: 5 minutes

Servings: 1

Nutritional Value per Serving:
- Calories: 200
- Protein: 10g
- Fiber: 4g
- Healthy Fats: 7g

Muesli with Fresh Berries and Almonds

Ingredients:

- 1/2 cup muesli
- 1/2 cup milk or almond milk
- 1/4 cup fresh berries
- 1 tbsp sliced almonds

Preparation:

1. In a bowl, combine muesli and milk.
2. Let sit for a few minutes to soften.
3. Top with fresh berries and sliced almonds.

Time to Prepare: 5 minutes

Servings: 1

Nutritional Value per Serving:

- Calories: 180
- Protein: 6g
- Fiber: 5g

- Healthy Fats: 6g

Nutritional Benefits

Each recipe in this chapter has been crafted to deliver essential nutrients that support seniors' health and vitality. Here are some key components:

- **Fiber**: Most of the breakfasts include whole grains, fruits, and vegetables, which add fiber to the diet. Fiber aids digestion, helps maintain blood sugar levels, and promotes fullness.
- **Healthy Fats**: Olive oil, nuts, seeds, and avocado provide unsaturated fats that support heart and brain health while offering sustained energy.
- **Protein**: Eggs, Greek yogurt, and legumes are included in many recipes to provide protein, which is essential for muscle maintenance and metabolic health.

By incorporating these nutritious breakfasts, seniors can enjoy a variety of flavors, textures, and nutrients each morning. These recipes emphasize balanced nutrition and Mediterranean flavors, setting a strong foundation for healthy aging.

Preview of Chapter 4: Lunches for Heart Health and Joint Support

In Chapter 4, we'll explore heart-healthy lunch recipes that are easy to prepare and include anti-inflammatory ingredients to support joint mobility. From hearty salads to nutrient-packed wraps, these lunches will provide sustained energy and essential nutrients for the day.

LUNCHES FOR HEART HEALTH AND JOINT SUPPORT

For seniors, lunchtime is an important opportunity to refuel with nutrient-dense foods that support both heart health and joint function. These recipes focus on ingredients rich in omega-3 fatty acids, fiber, antioxidants, and anti-inflammatory properties that contribute to cardiovascular health and reduce inflammation, which is often linked to joint discomfort and arthritis.

Key Nutrients and Ingredients for Heart and Joint Health

- **Omega-3 Fatty Acids**: Found in fish like tuna and salmon, as well as in walnuts and flaxseeds, omega-3s help reduce inflammation and protect the heart.

- **Fiber**: Fiber from whole grains, legumes, and vegetables supports digestion, helps regulate cholesterol, and stabilizes blood sugar levels.

- **Antioxidants**: Colorful vegetables like tomatoes, bell peppers, and leafy greens are packed with antioxidants that combat oxidative stress, which can contribute to inflammation.

- **Heart-Healthy Fats**: Olive oil, avocado, and nuts provide monounsaturated fats that support heart health and help reduce inflammation.

Recipes (30 Heart-Healthy Lunches)

Below are 30 Mediterranean-inspired lunch recipes, each designed to promote heart and joint health through nutritious ingredients and simple preparation steps. Each recipe includes ingredients, detailed steps, preparation time, servings, and nutritional information per serving.

Mediterranean Chickpea Salad with Lemon-Tahini Dressing

Ingredients:

- 1 cup canned chickpeas, rinsed and drained
- 1/2 cup cherry tomatoes, halved
- 1/4 cucumber, diced
- 1/4 red onion, finely diced
- 2 tbsp fresh parsley, chopped
- 2 tbsp tahini
- 1 tbsp lemon juice
- 1 tbsp olive oil

- Salt and pepper, to taste

Preparation:

1. In a bowl, combine chickpeas, cherry tomatoes, cucumber, red onion, and parsley.
2. In a small bowl, whisk together tahini, lemon juice, olive oil, salt, and pepper.
3. Pour the dressing over the salad and toss well to combine.
4. Serve immediately or refrigerate for 30 minutes to allow flavors to blend.

Time to Prepare: 10 minutes

Servings: 2

Nutritional Value per Serving:

- Calories: 220
- Protein: 7g
- Fiber: 6g
- Healthy Fats: 10g

Roasted Red Pepper Hummus Wrap

Ingredients:

- 1 whole-wheat tortilla
- 3 tbsp roasted red pepper hummus
- 1/4 cup shredded carrots
- 1/4 cucumber, thinly sliced
- 1/4 red bell pepper, thinly sliced
- Fresh spinach leaves

Preparation:

1. Spread the hummus evenly over the tortilla.
2. Layer carrots, cucumber, red bell pepper, and spinach leaves on top.
3. Roll the tortilla tightly, slice in half, and serve.

Time to Prepare: 5 minutes

Servings: 1

Nutritional Value per Serving:

- Calories: 200

- Protein: 6g
- Fiber: 5g
- Healthy Fats: 8g

Greek Lentil Salad with Feta

Ingredients:
- 1 cup cooked lentils
- 1/2 cup cherry tomatoes, halved
- 1/4 cup cucumber, diced
- 2 tbsp crumbled feta cheese
- 1 tbsp olive oil
- 1 tbsp lemon juice
- Salt and pepper, to taste
- Fresh oregano, chopped (optional)

Preparation:
1. In a large bowl, combine lentils, cherry tomatoes, cucumber, and feta cheese.
2. In a small bowl, whisk together olive oil, lemon juice, salt, and pepper.
3. Pour dressing over the salad, sprinkle with oregano, and toss to coat.

Time to Prepare: 10 minutes

Servings: 2

Nutritional Value per Serving:
- Calories: 210
- Protein: 9g
- Fiber: 7g
- Healthy Fats: 10g

Roasted Veggie and Quinoa Bowl

Ingredients:
- 1/2 cup cooked quinoa
- 1/4 cup roasted bell peppers
- 1/4 cup roasted zucchini
- 1/4 cup roasted eggplant
- 1 tbsp olive oil
- Salt and pepper, to taste
- Fresh basil leaves, for garnish

Preparation:
1. Arrange cooked quinoa in a bowl.
2. Top with roasted bell peppers, zucchini, and eggplant.
3. Drizzle with olive oil, season with salt and pepper, and garnish with fresh basil.

Time to Prepare: 10 minutes

Servings: 1

Nutritional Value per Serving:
- Calories: 220
- Protein: 6g
- Fiber: 5g
- Healthy Fats: 9g

Tuna Salad with Olives and Capers

Ingredients:
- 1 can (5 oz) tuna in water, drained
- 1 tbsp capers, rinsed
- 1/4 cup black olives, sliced
- 1 tbsp olive oil
- 1 tbsp lemon juice
- Fresh parsley, chopped

Preparation:

1. In a bowl, combine tuna, capers, and olives.
2. Drizzle with olive oil and lemon juice, then mix well.
3. Garnish with fresh parsley and serve.

Time to Prepare: 5 minutes

Servings: 2

Nutritional Value per Serving:

- Calories: 180
- Protein: 15g
- Fiber: 2g
- Healthy Fats: 8g

Avocado and Beet Salad

Ingredients:

- 1/2 avocado, diced
- 1/2 cup cooked beets, diced
- 1/4 cup arugula
- 1 tbsp balsamic vinegar
- 1 tbsp olive oil
- Salt and pepper, to taste

Preparation:

1. Arrange arugula in a bowl and top with diced avocado and beets.
2. Drizzle with balsamic vinegar and olive oil.
3. Season with salt and pepper, then toss gently to combine.

Time to Prepare: 5 minutes

Servings: 1

Nutritional Value per Serving:

- Calories: 210
- Protein: 3g
- Fiber: 6g

- Healthy Fats: 15g

Marinated White Bean and Tomato Salad

Ingredients:
- 1 cup canned white beans, rinsed and drained
- 1/2 cup cherry tomatoes, halved
- 1/4 red onion, finely diced
- 1 tbsp olive oil
- 1 tbsp red wine vinegar
- Salt and pepper, to taste
- Fresh basil, chopped

Preparation:
1. In a bowl, combine white beans, cherry tomatoes, and red onion.
2. In a small bowl, whisk together olive oil, red wine vinegar, salt, and pepper.
3. Pour dressing over the salad and sprinkle with fresh basil.

Time to Prepare: 10 minutes

Servings: 2

Nutritional Value per Serving:
- Calories: 190
- Protein: 8g
- Fiber: 6g
- Healthy Fats: 7g

Grilled Chicken Salad with Spinach and Olives

Ingredients:
- 1 cup fresh spinach leaves
- 1/4 cup cherry tomatoes, halved
- 1/4 cup cucumber, sliced
- 1/4 cup black olives, sliced

- 1/2 cup grilled chicken breast, sliced
- 1 tbsp olive oil
- 1 tbsp balsamic vinegar
- Salt and pepper, to taste

Preparation:

1. In a bowl, combine spinach, cherry tomatoes, cucumber, and olives.
2. Top with sliced grilled chicken.
3. Drizzle with olive oil and balsamic vinegar, season with salt and pepper, and toss lightly to coat.

Time to Prepare: 10 minutes

Servings: 2

Nutritional Value per Serving:

- Calories: 250
- Protein: 22g
- Fiber: 5g
- Healthy Fats: 10g

Farro and Roasted Vegetable Bowl

Ingredients:

- 1/2 cup cooked farro
- 1/4 cup roasted bell peppers
- 1/4 cup roasted zucchini
- 1/4 cup roasted carrots
- 1 tbsp olive oil
- Salt and pepper, to taste
- Fresh basil or parsley, chopped (optional)

Preparation:

1. Place cooked farro in a bowl.
2. Top with roasted vegetables, and drizzle with olive oil.
3. Season with salt and pepper, garnish with fresh herbs, and serve.

Time to Prepare: 10 minutes

Servings: 1

Nutritional Value per Serving:
- Calories: 230
- Protein: 7g
- Fiber: 6g
- Healthy Fats: 8g

Stuffed Pita with Tzatziki and Grilled Veggies

Ingredients:
- 1 whole-grain pita pocket
- 2 tbsp tzatziki sauce
- 1/4 cup grilled zucchini and eggplant
- Fresh spinach leaves

Preparation:
1. Cut the pita in half and gently open the pockets.

2. Spread tzatziki sauce inside each half.
3. Fill with grilled veggies and spinach leaves.
4. Serve immediately.

Time to Prepare: 5 minutes

Servings: 1

Nutritional Value per Serving:
- Calories: 200
- Protein: 6g
- Fiber: 5g
- Healthy Fats: 6g

Barley Salad with Roasted Butternut Squash

Ingredients:
- 1/2 cup cooked barley
- 1/4 cup roasted butternut squash, diced
- 1 tbsp crumbled feta cheese
- 1 tbsp chopped walnuts
- 1 tbsp olive oil
- 1 tsp balsamic vinegar
- Salt and pepper, to taste

Preparation:
1. In a bowl, combine cooked barley and roasted butternut squash.
2. Add feta cheese and walnuts.
3. Drizzle with olive oil and balsamic vinegar, season with salt and pepper, and toss to combine.

Time to Prepare: 10 minutes

Servings: 1

Nutritional Value per Serving:
- Calories: 260

- Protein: 8g
- Fiber: 7g
- Healthy Fats: 10g

Mediterranean Cabbage Slaw

Ingredients:
- 1 cup shredded cabbage
- 1/4 cup shredded carrots
- 1 tbsp chopped fresh parsley
- 1 tbsp olive oil
- 1 tbsp lemon juice
- Salt and pepper, to taste

Preparation:
1. In a large bowl, combine cabbage, carrots, and parsley.
2. Drizzle with olive oil and lemon juice.
3. Season with salt and pepper, then toss to combine.

Time to Prepare: 5 minutes

Servings: 2

Nutritional Value per Serving:
- Calories: 80
- Protein: 1g
- Fiber: 3g
- Healthy Fats: 7g

Lentil and Spinach Soup

Ingredients:
- 1/2 cup dried lentils, rinsed
- 2 cups vegetable broth
- 1/2 cup chopped spinach
- 1/4 onion, diced

- 1 clove garlic, minced
- 1 tbsp olive oil
- Salt and pepper, to taste

Preparation:

1. In a pot, heat olive oil over medium heat and sauté onion and garlic until softened.
2. Add lentils and vegetable broth, bring to a boil, then simmer for 20 minutes.
3. Add spinach, season with salt and pepper, and cook for an additional 5 minutes.

Time to Prepare: 30 minutes

Servings: 2

Nutritional Value per Serving:

- Calories: 180
- Protein: 10g
- Fiber: 8g
- Healthy Fats: 6g

Caprese Salad with Balsamic Reduction

Ingredients:

- 1 cup cherry tomatoes, halved
- 1/4 cup fresh mozzarella, cubed
- Fresh basil leaves
- 1 tbsp balsamic reduction
- Salt and pepper, to taste

Preparation:

1. In a bowl, combine cherry tomatoes and mozzarella.
2. Add basil leaves and drizzle with balsamic reduction.
3. Season with salt and pepper, then serve.

Time to Prepare: 5 minutes

Servings: 2

Nutritional Value per Serving:

- Calories: 120

- Protein: 6g
- Fiber: 2g
- Healthy Fats: 8g

Warm Mediterranean Grain Bowl

Ingredients:
- 1/2 cup cooked farro or quinoa
- 1/4 cup sautéed spinach
- 1/4 cup roasted cherry tomatoes
- 1 tbsp olive oil
- Salt and pepper, to taste
- Fresh herbs, chopped (optional)

Preparation:
1. Place cooked farro or quinoa in a bowl.
2. Add sautéed spinach and roasted cherry tomatoes.
3. Drizzle with olive oil, season with salt and pepper, and garnish with fresh herbs if desired.

Time to Prepare: 10 minutes

Servings: 1

Nutritional Value per Serving:
- Calories: 210
- Protein: 7g
- Fiber: 5g
- Healthy Fats: 8g

Couscous Salad with Feta and Cucumbers

Ingredients:
- 1/2 cup cooked couscous
- 1/4 cup cucumber, diced
- 1/4 cup crumbled feta cheese

- 1 tbsp olive oil
- 1 tbsp lemon juice
- Salt and pepper, to taste
- Fresh mint, chopped (optional)

Preparation:

1. In a large bowl, combine couscous, cucumber, and feta cheese.
2. Drizzle with olive oil and lemon juice.
3. Season with salt and pepper, and toss to combine.
4. Garnish with fresh mint, if desired.

Time to Prepare: 10 minutes

Servings: 2

Nutritional Value per Serving:
- Calories: 220
- Protein: 6g
- Fiber: 3g
- Healthy Fats: 9g

Kale and Cannellini Bean Salad

Ingredients:
- 1 cup kale, chopped
- 1/2 cup canned cannellini beans, drained and rinsed
- 1 tbsp olive oil
- 1 tbsp lemon juice
- 1/4 cup red onion, thinly sliced
- Salt and pepper, to taste

Preparation:

1. Massage chopped kale with olive oil and lemon juice until softened.
2. Add cannellini beans and red onion.
3. Season with salt and pepper, and toss to combine.

Time to Prepare: 5 minutes

Servings: 2

Nutritional Value per Serving:

- Calories: 180
- Protein: 8g
- Fiber: 7g
- Healthy Fats: 8g

Panzanella with Cherry Tomatoes and Basil

Ingredients:

- 1 cup whole-grain bread, cubed
- 1 cup cherry tomatoes, halved
- 1/4 red onion, thinly sliced
- Fresh basil leaves, torn
- 1 tbsp olive oil
- 1 tbsp red wine vinegar
- Salt and pepper, to taste

Preparation:

1. Toast the bread cubes until golden.
2. In a bowl, combine tomatoes, red onion, and basil.
3. Add toasted bread and drizzle with olive oil and red wine vinegar.
4. Season with salt and pepper, and toss to combine.

Time to Prepare: 10 minutes

Servings: 2

Nutritional Value per Serving:

- Calories: 200
- Protein: 6g
- Fiber: 5g
- Healthy Fats: 10g

Spiced Sweet Potato and Chickpea Bowl

Ingredients:
- 1 small sweet potato, cubed
- 1/2 cup canned chickpeas, rinsed and drained
- 1 tbsp olive oil
- 1/2 tsp cumin
- 1/4 tsp paprika
- Salt and pepper, to taste
- Fresh cilantro, for garnish

Preparation:
1. Preheat oven to 400°F (200°C).
2. Toss sweet potato and chickpeas with olive oil, cumin, paprika, salt, and pepper.
3. Spread on a baking sheet and roast for 20-25 minutes until golden and tender.
4. Garnish with fresh cilantro before serving.

Time to Prepare: 30 minutes

Servings: 2

Nutritional Value per Serving:
- Calories: 250
- Protein: 8g
- Fiber: 8g
- Healthy Fats: 9g

Warm Cauliflower and Chickpea Salad

Ingredients:
- 1 cup cauliflower florets
- 1/2 cup canned chickpeas, rinsed and drained
- 1 tbsp olive oil
- 1/2 tsp turmeric
- 1/4 tsp cumin
- Salt and pepper, to taste
- Fresh parsley, chopped

Preparation:
1. Preheat the oven to 400°F (200°C).
2. Toss cauliflower and chickpeas with olive oil, turmeric, cumin, salt, and pepper.
3. Roast on a baking sheet for 20-25 minutes, until cauliflower is tender.
4. Garnish with fresh parsley before serving.

Time to Prepare: 30 minutes

Servings: 2

Nutritional Value per Serving:

- Calories: 210
- Protein: 8g
- Fiber: 9g
- Healthy Fats: 8g

Fennel and Citrus Salad

Ingredients:

- 1/2 fennel bulb, thinly sliced
- 1 orange, peeled and sliced
- 1 tbsp olive oil
- 1 tbsp lemon juice
- Salt and pepper, to taste

Preparation:

1. In a bowl, combine fennel and orange slices.
2. Drizzle with olive oil and lemon juice.
3. Season with salt and pepper, and toss to combine.

Time to Prepare: 5 minutes

Servings: 2

Nutritional Value per Serving:

- Calories: 110
- Protein: 2g
- Fiber: 4g
- Healthy Fats: 8g

Grilled Vegetable Sandwich with Pesto

Ingredients:

- 1 whole-grain sandwich roll
- 1/2 cup grilled zucchini, sliced

- 1/4 cup roasted red pepper
- 1 tbsp pesto sauce
- Fresh arugula

Preparation:

1. Slice the sandwich roll and spread pesto on both sides.
2. Layer grilled zucchini, roasted red pepper, and arugula.
3. Serve immediately.

Time to Prepare: 10 minutes

Servings: 1

Nutritional Value per Serving:

- Calories: 250
- Protein: 7g
- Fiber: 6g
- Healthy Fats: 12g

Bulgur Salad with Fresh Herbs

Ingredients:

- 1/2 cup cooked bulgur
- 1/4 cup chopped fresh parsley
- 1/4 cup chopped fresh mint
- 1 tbsp olive oil
- 1 tbsp lemon juice
- Salt and pepper, to taste

Preparation:

1. Combine cooked bulgur with fresh parsley and mint.
2. Drizzle with olive oil and lemon juice.
3. Season with salt and pepper, and toss to combine.

Time to Prepare: 10 minutes

Servings: 2

Nutritional Value per Serving:

- Calories: 180
- Protein: 6g
- Fiber: 5g
- Healthy Fats: 7g

Roasted Beet and Walnut Salad

Ingredients:

- 1/2 cup roasted beets, diced
- 1/4 cup chopped walnuts
- 1 cup arugula
- 1 tbsp olive oil
- 1 tbsp balsamic vinegar
- Salt and pepper, to taste

Preparation:

1. In a bowl, combine roasted beets, walnuts, and arugula.
2. Drizzle with olive oil and balsamic vinegar.
3. Season with salt and pepper, and toss gently.

Time to Prepare: 10 minutes

Servings: 2

Nutritional Value per Serving:

- Calories: 210
- Protein: 5g
- Fiber: 6g
- Healthy Fats: 14g

Mediterranean-Style Tabouleh

Ingredients:

- 1/2 cup cooked bulgur

- 1 cup chopped parsley
- 1/4 cup diced tomatoes
- 1/4 cup diced cucumber
- 1 tbsp olive oil
- 1 tbsp lemon juice
- Salt and pepper, to taste

Preparation:

1. In a bowl, combine bulgur, parsley, tomatoes, and cucumber.
2. Drizzle with olive oil and lemon juice.
3. Season with salt and pepper, and toss to combine.

Time to Prepare: 10 minutes

Servings: 2

Nutritional Value per Serving:

- Calories: 180
- Protein: 5g
- Fiber: 7g
- Healthy Fats: 8g

Tuna and Cannellini Bean Salad

Ingredients:

- 1 can (5 oz) tuna in water, drained
- 1/2 cup canned cannellini beans, rinsed and drained
- 1 tbsp olive oil
- 1 tbsp lemon juice
- Salt and pepper, to taste
- Fresh parsley, chopped

Preparation:

1. In a bowl, combine tuna and cannellini beans.
2. Drizzle with olive oil and lemon juice.
3. Season with salt and pepper, and toss to combine.

4. Garnish with fresh parsley.

Time to Prepare: 5 minutes

Servings: 2

Nutritional Value per Serving:
- Calories: 220
- Protein: 24g
- Fiber: 6g
- Healthy Fats: 9g

Spinach and Mushroom Stuffed Bell Peppers

Ingredients:
- 2 large bell peppers, halved and seeded
- 1 cup fresh spinach, chopped
- 1/2 cup mushrooms, diced
- 1 tbsp olive oil
- Salt and pepper, to taste

Preparation:
1. Preheat oven to 375°F (190°C).
2. In a skillet, sauté spinach and mushrooms in olive oil until softened. Season with salt and pepper.
3. Stuff each bell pepper half with the spinach-mushroom mixture.
4. Bake for 20 minutes until bell peppers are tender.

Time to Prepare: 30 minutes

Servings: 2

Nutritional Value per Serving:
- Calories: 130
- Protein: 3g
- Fiber: 4g
- Healthy Fats: 7g

Carrot and Lentil Salad with Lemon Dressing

Ingredients:
- 1/2 cup cooked lentils
- 1/2 cup shredded carrots
- 1 tbsp olive oil
- 1 tbsp lemon juice
- Salt and pepper, to taste

Preparation:
1. In a bowl, combine lentils and carrots.
2. Drizzle with olive oil and lemon juice.
3. Season with salt and pepper, and toss to combine.

Time to Prepare: 5 minutes

Servings: 2

Nutritional Value per Serving:
- Calories: 160
- Protein: 7g
- Fiber: 7g
- Healthy Fats: 6g

Roasted Eggplant with Yogurt and Pomegranate

Ingredients:
- 1 small eggplant, sliced
- 1 tbsp olive oil
- Salt and pepper, to taste
- 1/4 cup Greek yogurt
- 2 tbsp pomegranate seeds
- Fresh mint, for garnish

Preparation:

1. Preheat oven to 400°F (200°C).
2. Brush eggplant slices with olive oil, season with salt and pepper, and roast for 20 minutes.
3. Top with Greek yogurt, sprinkle with pomegranate seeds, and garnish with mint.

Time to Prepare: 25 minutes

Servings: 2

Nutritional Value per Serving:
- Calories: 180
- Protein: 5g
- Fiber: 5g
- Healthy Fats: 9g

Mediterranean Chickpea and Spinach Stew

Ingredients:
- 1/2 cup canned chickpeas, rinsed and drained
- 1 cup fresh spinach
- 1/4 onion, diced
- 1 clove garlic, minced
- 1 cup vegetable broth
- 1 tbsp olive oil
- Salt and pepper, to taste

Preparation:

1. In a pot, heat olive oil over medium heat and sauté onion and garlic until softened.
2. Add chickpeas and vegetable broth, and bring to a simmer for 10 minutes.
3. Add spinach, season with salt and pepper, and cook for 2-3 minutes until wilted.

Time to Prepare: 15 minutes

Servings: 2

Nutritional Value per Serving:
- Calories: 160

- Protein: 7g
- Fiber: 6g
- Healthy Fats: 7g

Spinach and Mushroom Stuffed Bell Peppers

Ingredients:

- 2 large bell peppers, halved and seeded
- 1 cup fresh spinach, chopped
- 1/2 cup mushrooms, diced
- 1 tbsp olive oil
- Salt and pepper, to taste

Preparation:

1. Preheat oven to 375°F (190°C).
2. In a skillet, heat olive oil over medium heat and sauté spinach and mushrooms until softened. Season with salt and pepper.
3. Stuff each bell pepper half with the spinach-mushroom mixture.
4. Place the stuffed peppers on a baking sheet and bake for 20 minutes until the peppers are tender.

Time to Prepare: 30 minutes

Servings: 2

Nutritional Value per Serving:

- Calories: 130
- Protein: 3g
- Fiber: 4g
- Healthy Fats: 7g

Carrot and Lentil Salad with Lemon Dressing

Ingredients:

- 1/2 cup cooked lentils
- 1/2 cup shredded carrots

- 1 tbsp olive oil
- 1 tbsp lemon juice
- Salt and pepper, to taste
- Fresh parsley, chopped (optional)

Preparation:

1. In a bowl, combine lentils and shredded carrots.
2. Drizzle with olive oil and lemon juice.
3. Season with salt and pepper, and toss to combine.
4. Garnish with fresh parsley, if desired.

Time to Prepare: 5 minutes

Servings: 2

Nutritional Value per Serving:

- Calories: 160
- Protein: 7g
- Fiber: 7g
- Healthy Fats: 6g

Roasted Eggplant with Yogurt and Pomegranate

Ingredients:

- 1 small eggplant, sliced
- 1 tbsp olive oil
- Salt and pepper, to taste
- 1/4 cup Greek yogurt
- 2 tbsp pomegranate seeds
- Fresh mint leaves, for garnish

Preparation:

1. Preheat oven to 400°F (200°C).
2. Brush eggplant slices with olive oil and season with salt and pepper.
3. Arrange on a baking sheet and roast for 20 minutes until golden and tender.

4. Top each slice with a dollop of Greek yogurt, sprinkle with pomegranate seeds, and garnish with fresh mint.

Time to Prepare: 25 minutes

Servings: 2

Nutritional Value per Serving:
- Calories: 180
- Protein: 5g
- Fiber: 5g
- Healthy Fats: 9g

Mediterranean Chickpea and Spinach Stew

Ingredients:
- 1/2 cup canned chickpeas, rinsed and drained
- 1 cup fresh spinach
- 1/4 onion, diced
- 1 clove garlic, minced
- 1 cup low-sodium vegetable broth

- 1 tbsp olive oil
- Salt and pepper, to taste
- Fresh parsley, chopped (optional)

Preparation:

1. In a pot, heat olive oil over medium heat and sauté the onion and garlic until softened.
2. Add chickpeas and vegetable broth, and bring to a simmer for 10 minutes.
3. Stir in the spinach, season with salt and pepper, and cook for an additional 2-3 minutes until the spinach is wilted.
4. Garnish with fresh parsley, if desired, and serve warm.

Time to Prepare: 15 minutes

Servings: 2

Nutritional Value per Serving:

- Calories: 160
- Protein: 7g
- Fiber: 6g
- Healthy Fats: 7g

These heart-healthy, anti-inflammatory lunch recipes offer a range of flavors, textures, and nutrient-dense ingredients that support seniors' cardiovascular health and reduce joint inflammation. With a focus on Mediterranean flavors and fresh ingredients, each recipe can help seniors feel energized and nourished while benefiting overall health.

Preview of Chapter 5: Satisfying Dinners for Optimal Health and Sleep

In Chapter 5, we'll explore Mediterranean-inspired dinner recipes that are both satisfying and supportive of a restful night's sleep. These dishes will incorporate nutrient-rich ingredients that aid digestion and relaxation, providing seniors with meals that not only support their health but also promote restorative sleep.

DINNERS FOR BONE STRENGTH AND BRAIN HEALTH

Dinners rich in protein, calcium, and antioxidants play an essential role in supporting bone density, maintaining muscle mass, and protecting brain health. As we age, these nutrients become even more critical, as they help prevent osteoporosis, reduce inflammation, and promote mental clarity. These recipes incorporate key nutrients from a variety of Mediterranean-inspired ingredients, such as omega-3-rich fish, leafy greens, lean proteins, and antioxidant-packed vegetables.

Key Nutrients for Bone Strength and Brain Health

- **Calcium and Vitamin D**: Found in leafy greens, dairy, and fish, calcium and vitamin D help maintain strong bones and reduce the risk of fractures.

- **Omega-3 Fatty Acids**: Omega-3s from fatty fish and walnuts reduce inflammation, promote brain health, and support cognitive function.

- **Antioxidants**: Found in colorful vegetables like bell peppers, tomatoes, and spinach, antioxidants help protect brain cells from oxidative stress.

- **Protein**: Lean protein from chicken, fish, legumes, and tofu helps maintain muscle mass, supports bone structure, and contributes to satiety.

Recipes (30 Brain- and Bone-Supporting Dinners)

Below are 30 Mediterranean-inspired dinner recipes designed to support both bone strength and brain health. Each recipe includes ingredients, detailed steps, preparation time, servings, and nutritional information per serving.

Grilled Salmon with Asparagus and Lemon

Ingredients:

- 1 salmon fillet (4 oz)
- 1/2 bunch asparagus, trimmed
- 1 tbsp olive oil
- Salt and pepper, to taste
- 1/2 lemon, sliced

Preparation:

1. Preheat the grill to medium-high heat.
2. Drizzle salmon and asparagus with olive oil, and season with salt and pepper.
3. Grill salmon and asparagus for 4-5 minutes per side, or until cooked through.

4. Serve with lemon slices.

Time to Prepare: 15 minutes

Servings: 1

Nutritional Value per Serving:
- Calories: 290
- Protein: 25g
- Omega-3 Fats: 1.5g
- Calcium: 30mg

Baked Chicken with Olives and Artichokes

Ingredients:
- 1 chicken breast, boneless and skinless
- 1/4 cup black olives, pitted
- 1/4 cup artichoke hearts, chopped
- 1 tbsp olive oil
- 1/2 lemon, juiced
- Salt and pepper, to taste

Preparation:
1. Preheat oven to 375°F (190°C).
2. Place chicken breast in a baking dish and top with olives and artichokes.
3. Drizzle with olive oil and lemon juice, then season with salt and pepper.
4. Bake for 25-30 minutes or until chicken is cooked through.

Time to Prepare: 30 minutes

Servings: 1

Nutritional Value per Serving:
- Calories: 280
- Protein: 26g
- Calcium: 20mg
- Healthy Fats: 14g

Ratatouille with Zucchini and Eggplant

Ingredients:
- 1/2 zucchini, sliced
- 1/2 eggplant, diced
- 1/2 red bell pepper, sliced
- 1/4 cup cherry tomatoes
- 1 tbsp olive oil
- 1 clove garlic, minced
- Fresh basil, chopped (for garnish)
- Salt and pepper, to taste

Preparation:
1. Preheat oven to 400°F (200°C).
2. In a baking dish, combine zucchini, eggplant, bell pepper, tomatoes, olive oil, and garlic.
3. Season with salt and pepper, then toss to coat.
4. Roast for 20-25 minutes, or until vegetables are tender. Garnish with basil.

Time to Prepare: 30 minutes

Servings: 2

Nutritional Value per Serving:
- Calories: 140
- Protein: 3g
- Fiber: 6g
- Calcium: 30mg

Mediterranean Stuffed Peppers

Ingredients:

- 2 bell peppers, halved and seeded
- 1/2 cup cooked quinoa
- 1/4 cup diced tomatoes
- 1/4 cup chickpeas, rinsed and drained
- 1 tbsp crumbled feta cheese
- Salt and pepper, to taste

Preparation:

1. Preheat oven to 375°F (190°C).
2. In a bowl, combine quinoa, tomatoes, chickpeas, and feta cheese.
3. Fill each pepper half with the quinoa mixture.
4. Place in a baking dish, cover with foil, and bake for 25-30 minutes.

Time to Prepare: 35 minutes

Servings: 2

Nutritional Value per Serving:

- Calories: 200
- Protein: 7g
- Fiber: 5g
- Calcium: 70mg

Lemon Herb Shrimp Skewers

Ingredients:

- 6 large shrimp, peeled and deveined
- 1 tbsp olive oil
- 1/2 lemon, juiced
- 1 tsp chopped fresh parsley
- Salt and pepper, to taste

Preparation:

1. Preheat the grill to medium-high heat.

2. In a bowl, combine olive oil, lemon juice, parsley, salt, and pepper.
3. Thread shrimp onto skewers and brush with the lemon-herb mixture.
4. Grill for 2-3 minutes per side or until shrimp are pink and cooked through.

Time to Prepare: 10 minutes

Servings: 1

Nutritional Value per Serving:
- Calories: 150
- Protein: 15g
- Omega-3 Fats: 0.4g
- Calcium: 80mg

Spinach and Feta-Stuffed Chicken

Ingredients:
- 1 chicken breast, boneless and skinless
- 1/4 cup fresh spinach, chopped
- 2 tbsp feta cheese, crumbled
- 1 tbsp olive oil
- Salt and pepper, to taste

Preparation:
1. Preheat oven to 375°F (190°C).
2. Slice a pocket into the side of the chicken breast.
3. Stuff the pocket with spinach and feta, then secure with toothpicks.
4. Drizzle with olive oil, season with salt and pepper, and bake for 25-30 minutes.

Time to Prepare: 30 minutes

Servings: 1

Nutritional Value per Serving:
- Calories: 270
- Protein: 30g
- Calcium: 100mg
- Healthy Fats: 12g

Eggplant Parmesan with Whole-Grain Pasta

Ingredients:

- 1 small eggplant, sliced
- 1/2 cup marinara sauce
- 1/4 cup shredded mozzarella cheese
- 1/2 cup cooked whole-grain pasta
- Salt and pepper, to taste

Preparation:

1. Preheat oven to 375°F (190°C).
2. Arrange eggplant slices on a baking sheet, season with salt and pepper, and bake for 10 minutes.
3. Top each slice with marinara sauce and mozzarella cheese, then bake for another 10 minutes.
4. Serve with whole-grain pasta.

Time to Prepare: 25 minutes

Servings: 2

Nutritional Value per Serving:

- Calories: 240
- Protein: 8g
- Fiber: 6g
- Calcium: 120mg

Greek Beef Kofta with Tzatziki

Ingredients:

- 1/4 lb ground beef
- 1 clove garlic, minced
- 1/2 tsp cumin
- 1/2 tsp paprika
- Salt and pepper, to taste
- 2 tbsp tzatziki sauce
- Fresh parsley, for garnish

Preparation:

1. In a bowl, mix ground beef, garlic, cumin, paprika, salt, and pepper.
2. Form into small, oblong patties.
3. Grill or pan-fry the kofta for 4-5 minutes per side.
4. Serve with tzatziki sauce and garnish with parsley.

Time to Prepare: 15 minutes

Servings: 2

Nutritional Value per Serving:

- Calories: 220
- Protein: 15g
- Calcium: 40mg
- Healthy Fats: 12g

Roasted Cod with Olive Tapenade

Ingredients:

- 1 cod fillet (4 oz)
- 1 tbsp olive tapenade
- 1 tbsp olive oil
- Salt and pepper, to taste
- Fresh parsley, chopped (optional)

Preparation:

1. Preheat oven to 400°F (200°C).
2. Place cod fillet on a baking sheet and brush with olive oil.
3. Spread olive tapenade over the fillet, and season with salt and pepper.
4. Roast for 12-15 minutes, until fish is flaky and cooked through.
5. Garnish with fresh parsley if desired.

Time to Prepare: 15 minutes

Servings: 1

Nutritional Value per Serving:

- Calories: 210
- Protein: 24g
- Omega-3 Fats: 1g
- Calcium: 30mg

Lentil and Vegetable Stew

Ingredients:

- 1/2 cup dried lentils, rinsed
- 1 cup vegetable broth
- 1/4 cup diced carrots
- 1/4 cup diced celery
- 1/4 cup diced tomatoes
- 1 tbsp olive oil
- Salt and pepper, to taste
- Fresh thyme or rosemary (optional)

Preparation:

1. In a pot, heat olive oil over medium heat and sauté carrots and celery until softened.
2. Add lentils, vegetable broth, and diced tomatoes.
3. Season with salt, pepper, and add fresh herbs if desired.
4. Simmer for 25-30 minutes, until lentils are tender.

Time to Prepare: 35 minutes

Servings: 2

Nutritional Value per Serving:
- Calories: 250
- Protein: 12g
- Fiber: 8g
- Calcium: 40mg

Chicken Souvlaki with Tabbouleh

Ingredients:
- 1 chicken breast, cubed
- 1 tbsp olive oil
- 1/2 lemon, juiced
- Salt and pepper, to taste
- 1/2 cup cooked bulgur
- 1/4 cup diced tomatoes
- 1/4 cup chopped parsley
- 1 tbsp olive oil (for tabbouleh)
- 1 tbsp lemon juice (for tabbouleh)

Preparation:
1. In a bowl, marinate chicken with olive oil, lemon juice, salt, and pepper.
2. Grill or pan-fry chicken for 5-7 minutes until cooked through.
3. In another bowl, combine bulgur, tomatoes, parsley, olive oil, and lemon juice.
4. Serve grilled chicken with tabbouleh.

Time to Prepare: 20 minutes

Servings: 2

Nutritional Value per Serving:

- Calories: 320
- Protein: 25g
- Calcium: 30mg
- Healthy Fats: 14g

Pasta Primavera with Fresh Herbs

Ingredients:

- 1/2 cup whole-grain pasta, cooked
- 1/4 cup cherry tomatoes, halved
- 1/4 cup zucchini, sliced
- 1 tbsp olive oil
- Fresh basil and parsley, chopped
- Salt and pepper, to taste

Preparation:

1. In a skillet, heat olive oil over medium heat and sauté zucchini until tender.
2. Add cherry tomatoes and cooked pasta, stirring until heated through.
3. Season with salt, pepper, and fresh herbs.

Time to Prepare: 15 minutes

Servings: 2

Nutritional Value per Serving:

- Calories: 210
- Protein: 6g
- Fiber: 6g
- Calcium: 25mg

Chickpea and Spinach Stew

Ingredients:

- 1/2 cup canned chickpeas, rinsed and drained
- 1 cup fresh spinach

- 1/4 onion, diced
- 1 clove garlic, minced
- 1 cup vegetable broth
- 1 tbsp olive oil
- Salt and pepper, to taste

Preparation:

1. In a pot, heat olive oil over medium heat and sauté onion and garlic until softened.
2. Add chickpeas, spinach, and vegetable broth.
3. Season with salt and pepper and simmer for 10 minutes.

Time to Prepare: 15 minutes

Servings: 2

Nutritional Value per Serving:

- Calories: 180
- Protein: 7g
- Fiber: 5g
- Calcium: 60mg

Stuffed Zucchini Boats

Ingredients:

- 1 medium zucchini, halved and seeded
- 1/4 cup cooked quinoa
- 2 tbsp diced tomatoes
- 1 tbsp crumbled feta cheese
- Salt and pepper, to taste

Preparation:

1. Preheat oven to 375°F (190°C).
2. In a bowl, combine quinoa, tomatoes, and feta cheese.
3. Stuff zucchini halves with the mixture.
4. Place on a baking sheet and bake for 15-20 minutes.

Time to Prepare: 25 minutes

Servings: 2

Nutritional Value per Serving:
- Calories: 120
- Protein: 4g
- Fiber: 4g
- Calcium: 45mg

Grilled Mackerel with Roasted Vegetables

Ingredients:
- 1 mackerel fillet (4 oz)
- 1/2 cup cherry tomatoes
- 1/4 cup sliced zucchini
- 1 tbsp olive oil
- Salt and pepper, to taste
- Fresh parsley, chopped (optional)

Preparation:
1. Preheat grill to medium heat.
2. Drizzle mackerel and vegetables with olive oil, and season with salt and pepper.
3. Grill mackerel for 4-5 minutes per side and roast vegetables in the oven at 400°F (200°C) for 15 minutes.
4. Serve together with fresh parsley if desired.

Time to Prepare: 20 minutes

Servings: 1

Nutritional Value per Serving:
- Calories: 230
- Protein: 21g
- Omega-3 Fats: 1.3g
- Calcium: 40mg

Garlic Shrimp with Couscous

Ingredients:

- 6 large shrimp, peeled and deveined
- 1 clove garlic, minced
- 1 tbsp olive oil
- 1/2 cup cooked couscous
- Salt and pepper, to taste
- Fresh parsley, chopped

Preparation:

1. Heat olive oil in a skillet over medium heat.
2. Add garlic and shrimp, cooking until shrimp are pink and cooked through (about 2-3 minutes).
3. Serve over couscous and garnish with fresh parsley.

Time to Prepare: 10 minutes

Servings: 1

Nutritional Value per Serving:

- Calories: 180
- Protein: 15g
- Calcium: 60mg
- Healthy Fats: 8g

Spaghetti Squash with Marinara

Ingredients:

- 1 small spaghetti squash, halved and seeded
- 1/2 cup marinara sauce
- 1 tbsp grated Parmesan cheese
- Salt and pepper, to taste

Preparation:

1. Preheat oven to 400°F (200°C).
2. Place squash halves cut-side down on a baking sheet and roast for 25-30 minutes until tender.

3. Scrape the inside with a fork to create spaghetti-like strands.
4. Top with marinara sauce and Parmesan.

Time to Prepare: 30 minutes

Servings: 2

Nutritional Value per Serving:
- Calories: 120
- Protein: 4g
- Fiber: 5g
- Calcium: 40mg

Lamb Meatballs with Yogurt Sauce

Ingredients:
- 1/4 lb ground lamb
- 1 clove garlic, minced
- Salt and pepper, to taste
- 2 tbsp Greek yogurt
- 1/2 tsp lemon juice
- Fresh mint, chopped (optional)

Preparation:
1. In a bowl, mix ground lamb, garlic, salt, and pepper, and form into small meatballs.
2. Pan-fry or bake meatballs for 10 minutes, until cooked through.
3. In a separate bowl, combine yogurt, lemon juice, and mint.
4. Serve meatballs with yogurt sauce.

Time to Prepare: 15 minutes

Servings: 2

Nutritional Value per Serving:
- Calories: 250
- Protein: 16g
- Calcium: 50mg

- Healthy Fats: 16g

Stuffed Eggplant with Ground Turkey

Ingredients:

- 1 small eggplant, halved and seeded
- 1/4 lb ground turkey
- 1/4 cup diced tomatoes
- 1 tbsp olive oil
- Salt and pepper, to taste
- Fresh basil, chopped (optional)

Preparation:

1. Preheat oven to 375°F (190°C).
2. In a skillet, cook ground turkey with olive oil until browned. Add tomatoes, salt, and pepper.
3. Spoon turkey mixture into the eggplant halves.
4. Place on a baking sheet and bake for 25 minutes.

Time to Prepare: 30 minutes

Servings: 2

Nutritional Value per Serving:

- Calories: 220
- Protein: 14g
- Calcium: 40mg
- Healthy Fats: 10g

Poached Cod with Saffron

Ingredients:

- 1 cod fillet (4 oz)
- 1 cup vegetable broth
- 1 pinch saffron threads
- Salt and pepper, to taste
- Fresh parsley, for garnish

Preparation:

1. In a skillet, heat vegetable broth and saffron over medium heat.
2. Add cod fillet and poach for 8-10 minutes until flaky.
3. Season with salt and pepper and garnish with parsley.

Time to Prepare: 15 minutes

Servings: 1

Nutritional Value per Serving:

- Calories: 180
- Protein: 22g

- Calcium: 20mg
- Healthy Fats: 5g

Mushroom and Leek Risotto

Ingredients:

- 1/2 cup Arborio rice
- 1 cup low-sodium vegetable broth
- 1/2 cup mushrooms, sliced
- 1/2 leek, sliced
- 1 tbsp olive oil
- Salt and pepper, to taste
- Fresh parsley, for garnish

Preparation:

1. In a pot, heat olive oil over medium heat and sauté mushrooms and leeks until softened.
2. Add Arborio rice and stir for 1-2 minutes.
3. Gradually add vegetable broth, stirring until absorbed, until rice is tender (about 15-20 minutes).
4. Season with salt and pepper and garnish with fresh parsley.

Time to Prepare: 25 minutes

Servings: 2

Nutritional Value per Serving:

- Calories: 220
- Protein: 5g
- Fiber: 3g
- Calcium: 25mg

Greek-Style Baked Fish

Ingredients:

- 1 white fish fillet (such as tilapia or cod, 4 oz)
- 1/4 cup cherry tomatoes, halved

- 1/4 red onion, thinly sliced
- 1 tbsp olive oil
- 1/2 lemon, juiced
- Fresh oregano, chopped
- Salt and pepper, to taste

Preparation:

1. Preheat oven to 375°F (190°C).
2. Place fish fillet in a baking dish and top with tomatoes and onion.
3. Drizzle with olive oil and lemon juice, season with salt, pepper, and oregano.
4. Bake for 15-18 minutes until fish is cooked through.

Time to Prepare: 20 minutes

Servings: 1

Nutritional Value per Serving:

- Calories: 190
- Protein: 22g
- Calcium: 30mg
- Healthy Fats: 9g

Cauliflower and Broccoli Stir-Fry

Ingredients:

- 1 cup cauliflower florets
- 1 cup broccoli florets
- 1 clove garlic, minced
- 1 tbsp olive oil
- Salt and pepper, to taste
- 1 tbsp soy sauce (optional)

Preparation:

1. In a skillet, heat olive oil over medium heat and sauté garlic until fragrant.
2. Add cauliflower and broccoli and stir-fry until tender-crisp, about 5-7 minutes.

3. Season with salt, pepper, and soy sauce if desired.

Time to Prepare: 10 minutes

Servings: 2

Nutritional Value per Serving:
- Calories: 110
- Protein: 4g
- Fiber: 5g
- Calcium: 35mg

Baked Ratatouille with Feta

Ingredients:
- 1/2 zucchini, sliced
- 1/2 eggplant, sliced
- 1/2 red bell pepper, sliced
- 1/4 cup cherry tomatoes
- 1 tbsp olive oil
- 2 tbsp crumbled feta cheese
- Salt and pepper, to taste
- Fresh basil, for garnish

Preparation:
1. Preheat oven to 375°F (190°C).
2. In a baking dish, layer zucchini, eggplant, bell pepper, and cherry tomatoes.
3. Drizzle with olive oil, season with salt and pepper, and bake for 20 minutes.
4. Sprinkle with feta cheese and bake for an additional 5 minutes. Garnish with basil.

Time to Prepare: 25 minutes

Servings: 2

Nutritional Value per Serving:
- Calories: 140
- Protein: 4g
- Fiber: 4g

- Calcium: 70mg

Sautéed Swiss Chard with Garlic and Lemon

Ingredients:

- 1 cup Swiss chard, chopped
- 1 clove garlic, minced
- 1 tbsp olive oil
- 1/2 lemon, juiced
- Salt and pepper, to taste

Preparation:

1. Heat olive oil in a skillet over medium heat and sauté garlic until fragrant.
2. Add Swiss chard and cook until wilted, about 3-4 minutes.
3. Drizzle with lemon juice, season with salt and pepper, and serve.

Time to Prepare: 5 minutes

Servings: 2

Nutritional Value per Serving:

- Calories: 80
- Protein: 2g
- Fiber: 2g
- Calcium: 50mg

Zucchini Noodles with Tomato Basil Sauce

Ingredients:

- 1 large zucchini, spiralized into noodles
- 1/2 cup marinara sauce
- Fresh basil leaves, chopped
- 1 tbsp olive oil
- Salt and pepper, to taste

Preparation:

1. In a skillet, heat olive oil over medium heat and add zucchini noodles.
2. Sauté for 2-3 minutes until tender.
3. Add marinara sauce and cook for another 1-2 minutes.
4. Season with salt, pepper, and top with fresh basil.

Time to Prepare: 10 minutes

Servings: 2

Nutritional Value per Serving:

- Calories: 90
- Protein: 2g
- Fiber: 3g
- Calcium: 25mg

Moroccan Chickpea and Carrot Tagine

Ingredients:

- 1/2 cup canned chickpeas, rinsed and drained
- 1/2 cup carrots, sliced
- 1/4 onion, diced
- 1 tbsp olive oil
- 1/2 tsp ground cumin
- 1/4 tsp ground cinnamon
- Salt and pepper, to taste

Preparation:

1. Heat olive oil in a pot over medium heat and sauté onions and carrots until softened.
2. Add chickpeas, cumin, cinnamon, salt, and pepper.
3. Simmer for 10 minutes until flavors meld together.

Time to Prepare: 15 minutes

Servings: 2

Nutritional Value per Serving:

- Calories: 150
- Protein: 5g
- Fiber: 5g
- Calcium: 30mg

Grilled Lamb Chops with Rosemary

Ingredients:
- 2 small lamb chops
- 1 tbsp olive oil
- 1 tsp fresh rosemary, chopped
- Salt and pepper, to taste

Preparation:
1. Preheat grill to medium-high heat.
2. Brush lamb chops with olive oil, and season with rosemary, salt, and pepper.
3. Grill lamb chops for 3-4 minutes per side, until desired doneness is reached.

Time to Prepare: 10 minutes

Servings: 2

Nutritional Value per Serving:
- Calories: 250
- Protein: 20g
- Calcium: 20mg
- Healthy Fats: 15g

Baked Eggplant with Mozzarella

Ingredients:
- 1 small eggplant, sliced
- 1/4 cup marinara sauce
- 1/4 cup shredded mozzarella cheese
- Salt and pepper, to taste
- Fresh basil, for garnish

Preparation:

1. Preheat oven to 375°F (190°C).
2. Arrange eggplant slices on a baking sheet and season with salt and pepper.
3. Top each slice with marinara sauce and mozzarella cheese.
4. Bake for 15-20 minutes, until cheese is melted and bubbly. Garnish with basil.

Time to Prepare: 20 minutes

Servings: 2

Nutritional Value per Serving:

- Calories: 180
- Protein: 6g
- Fiber: 4g
- Calcium: 80mg

Artichoke and Spinach Bake

Ingredients:

- 1/2 cup canned artichoke hearts, chopped

- 1 cup fresh spinach, chopped
- 1/4 cup Greek yogurt
- 1/4 cup shredded mozzarella cheese
- Salt and pepper, to taste

Preparation:

1. Preheat oven to 375°F (190°C).
2. In a bowl, combine artichoke hearts, spinach, Greek yogurt, and mozzarella cheese.
3. Season with salt and pepper, then transfer mixture to a baking dish.
4. Bake for 15-20 minutes, until cheese is melted and golden.

Time to Prepare: 20 minutes

Servings: 2

Nutritional Value per Serving:

- Calories: 160
- Protein: 9g
- Fiber: 3g
- Calcium: 100mg

These Mediterranean-inspired dinners offer a variety of nutrient-dense ingredients that support bone strength, brain health, and overall wellness. Each dish emphasizes the benefits of calcium, omega-3 fatty acids, antioxidants, and lean proteins to promote cognitive and physical well-being for seniors.

Preview of Chapter 6: Light and Satisfying Salads for Every Day

In Chapter 6, we'll explore a selection of light and flavorful salads perfect for any time of day. These salads are rich in antioxidants, fiber, and healthy fats, offering refreshing and nourishing options

NUTRIENT-DENSE SNACKS AND SMALL PLATES

Snacks in the Mediterranean diet aren't just "fillers" between meals; they're an essential way to fuel the body with nutrient-dense foods that promote long-term health. These snacks are easy to prepare and include whole ingredients, such as fresh vegetables, lean proteins, healthy fats, and whole grains, that satisfy hunger and support digestive and heart health.

Key Nutrients for Energy and Satiety

- **Fiber**: Helps with satiety, digestion, and blood sugar control. Found in vegetables, whole grains, nuts, and seeds.

- **Healthy Fats**: Monounsaturated fats from olives, nuts, and avocados contribute to heart health and keep you feeling full longer.

- **Natural Protein**: High-protein snacks like Greek yogurt, cottage cheese, and nuts maintain muscle mass and support blood sugar stability.

Recipes (30 Nutritious Snacks)

Below are 30 Mediterranean-inspired snack recipes designed to provide stable energy and prevent hunger. Each recipe includes ingredients, detailed steps, preparation time, servings, and nutritional information per serving.

Olive Tapenade with Whole-Grain Crackers

Ingredients:

- 1/2 cup black olives, pitted
- 1 tbsp capers
- 1 clove garlic, minced
- 1 tbsp olive oil
- Whole-grain crackers for serving

Preparation:

1. In a food processor, blend olives, capers, garlic, and olive oil until smooth.
2. Serve with whole-grain crackers.

Time to Prepare: 5 minutes

Servings: 2

Nutritional Value per Serving:

- Calories: 120
- Protein: 2g
- Fiber: 2g

- Healthy Fats: 10g

Greek Yogurt Dip with Cucumber Slices

Ingredients:

- 1/2 cup Greek yogurt
- 1 tbsp fresh dill, chopped
- 1/2 clove garlic, minced
- Salt and pepper, to taste
- Cucumber slices for dipping

Preparation:

1. In a bowl, mix Greek yogurt, dill, garlic, salt, and pepper.
2. Serve with cucumber slices.

Time to Prepare: 5 minutes

Servings: 2

Nutritional Value per Serving:

- Calories: 80
- Protein: 6g
- Fiber: 1g
- Healthy Fats: 1g

Baked Zucchini Chips with Parmesan

Ingredients:

- 1 zucchini, thinly sliced
- 1 tbsp olive oil
- 1 tbsp grated Parmesan cheese
- Salt and pepper, to taste

Preparation:

1. Preheat oven to 400°F (200°C).
2. Toss zucchini slices with olive oil, Parmesan, salt, and pepper.

3. Spread on a baking sheet and bake for 15-20 minutes until crispy.

Time to Prepare: 20 minutes

Servings: 2

Nutritional Value per Serving:
- Calories: 70
- Protein: 3g
- Fiber: 1g
- Healthy Fats: 5g

Fresh Veggies with Hummus

Ingredients:
- 1/2 cup hummus
- Fresh veggies (carrot sticks, bell pepper slices, cucumber) for dipping

Preparation:
1. Serve hummus with a variety of fresh veggies.

Time to Prepare: 2 minutes

Servings: 2

Nutritional Value per Serving:
- Calories: 100
- Protein: 3g
- Fiber: 3g
- Healthy Fats: 6g

Roasted Spiced Chickpeas

Ingredients:
- 1/2 cup canned chickpeas, rinsed and drained
- 1 tsp olive oil
- 1/4 tsp paprika
- Salt and pepper, to taste

Preparation:

1. Preheat oven to 400°F (200°C).
2. Toss chickpeas with olive oil, paprika, salt, and pepper.
3. Spread on a baking sheet and roast for 15-20 minutes until crispy.

Time to Prepare: 20 minutes

Servings: 2

Nutritional Value per Serving:
- Calories: 90
- Protein: 4g
- Fiber: 3g
- Healthy Fats: 4g

Marinated Olives with Feta Cubes

Ingredients:
- 1/4 cup mixed olives
- 2 tbsp feta cheese, cubed
- 1 tsp olive oil
- Fresh herbs (rosemary, thyme) for garnish

Preparation:
1. Combine olives, feta, and olive oil in a small bowl.
2. Garnish with fresh herbs and serve.

Time to Prepare: 5 minutes

Servings: 2

Nutritional Value per Serving:
- Calories: 110
- Protein: 3g
- Fiber: 1g
- Healthy Fats: 10g

Dates Stuffed with Almonds and Ricotta

Ingredients:

- 4 Medjool dates, pitted
- 4 almonds
- 2 tbsp ricotta cheese

Preparation:

1. Fill each date with 1 almond and a small amount of ricotta cheese.
2. Serve immediately.

Time to Prepare: 5 minutes

Servings: 2

Nutritional Value per Serving:

- Calories: 100
- Protein: 2g
- Fiber: 2g
- Healthy Fats: 3g

Almond Butter on Apple Slices

Ingredients:

- 1 apple, sliced
- 1 tbsp almond butter

Preparation:

1. Spread almond butter on apple slices.
2. Serve as a quick and easy snack.

Time to Prepare: 2 minutes

Servings: 1

Nutritional Value per Serving:

- Calories: 150
- Protein: 2g
- Fiber: 4g
- Healthy Fats: 8g

Caprese Skewers with Cherry Tomatoes and Mozzarella

Ingredients:

- 6 cherry tomatoes
- 6 small mozzarella balls
- Fresh basil leaves
- Balsamic vinegar for drizzling

Preparation:

1. Skewer cherry tomatoes, mozzarella, and basil leaves.
2. Drizzle with balsamic vinegar.

Time to Prepare: 5 minutes

Servings: 2

Nutritional Value per Serving:

- Calories: 90
- Protein: 5g
- Fiber: 1g
- Healthy Fats: 6g

Whole-Wheat Pita with Tzatziki

Ingredients:

- 1 small whole-wheat pita, cut into triangles
- 1/4 cup tzatziki

Preparation:

1. Serve pita triangles with tzatziki dip.

Time to Prepare: 2 minutes

Servings: 1

Nutritional Value per Serving:

- Calories: 130
- Protein: 4g
- Fiber: 3g
- Healthy Fats: 5g

Stuffed Grape Leaves

Ingredients:

- 8 grape leaves, rinsed

- 1/4 cup cooked rice
- 1 tbsp pine nuts
- 1 tbsp chopped parsley
- 1/2 lemon, juiced

Preparation:

1. In a bowl, mix rice, pine nuts, parsley, and lemon juice.
2. Place a spoonful of the mixture in each grape leaf and roll tightly.
3. Serve chilled or at room temperature.

Time to Prepare: 10 minutes

Servings: 2

Nutritional Value per Serving:

- Calories: 90
- Protein: 2g
- Fiber: 1g
- Healthy Fats: 3g

Cucumber Rounds with Smoked Salmon

Ingredients:

- 1 cucumber, sliced into rounds
- 2 oz smoked salmon
- 1 tbsp cream cheese
- Fresh dill, for garnish

Preparation:

1. Spread a small amount of cream cheese on each cucumber round.
2. Top with a piece of smoked salmon and garnish with dill.

Time to Prepare: 5 minutes

Servings: 2

Nutritional Value per Serving:

- Calories: 70
- Protein: 6g

- Fiber: 1g
- Healthy Fats: 3g

Sweet Potato Toast with Avocado and Tomato

Ingredients:

- 1 small sweet potato, sliced into thin rounds
- 1/4 avocado, sliced
- 1 cherry tomato, sliced
- Salt and pepper, to taste

Preparation:

1. Toast sweet potato slices in a toaster or oven until tender.
2. Top with avocado and tomato slices, season with salt and pepper.

Time to Prepare: 10 minutes

Servings: 1

Nutritional Value per Serving:

- Calories: 110
- Protein: 2g
- Fiber: 4g
- Healthy Fats: 5g

Greek Yogurt with Honey and Walnuts

Ingredients:

- 1/2 cup Greek yogurt
- 1 tsp honey
- 1 tbsp chopped walnuts

Preparation:

1. Place Greek yogurt in a bowl.
2. Drizzle with honey and sprinkle with walnuts.

Time to Prepare: 2 minutes

Servings: 1

Nutritional Value per Serving:
- Calories: 150
- Protein: 8g
- Fiber: 1g
- Healthy Fats: 7g

Cottage Cheese with Pineapple and Mint

Ingredients:
- 1/2 cup cottage cheese
- 1/4 cup fresh pineapple, diced
- Fresh mint leaves, chopped

Preparation:
1. Place cottage cheese in a bowl and top with pineapple.
2. Garnish with fresh mint.

Time to Prepare: 3 minutes

Servings: 1

Nutritional Value per Serving:
- Calories: 100
- Protein: 10g
- Fiber: 1g
- Healthy Fats: 2g

Mini Greek Salad Cups

Ingredients:
- 1/4 cup diced cucumber
- 1/4 cup cherry tomatoes, halved
- 1 tbsp crumbled feta cheese
- 1/4 cup romaine lettuce, chopped
- 1 tbsp olive oil

- Salt and pepper, to taste

Preparation:

1. Layer ingredients in small cups, starting with lettuce, followed by cucumber, tomatoes, and feta.
2. Drizzle with olive oil and season with salt and pepper.

Time to Prepare: 5 minutes

Servings: 2

Nutritional Value per Serving:

- Calories: 80
- Protein: 2g
- Fiber: 2g
- Healthy Fats: 6g

Almond and Fig Energy Bites

Ingredients:

- 1/4 cup almonds
- 2 dried figs
- 1/2 tsp cinnamon

Preparation:

1. In a food processor, blend almonds, figs, and cinnamon until combined.
2. Roll into small bites and refrigerate for 10 minutes.

Time to Prepare: 10 minutes

Servings: 2

Nutritional Value per Serving:

- Calories: 90
- Protein: 2g
- Fiber: 2g
- Healthy Fats: 5g

Roasted Red Pepper and Walnut Dip

Ingredients:

- 1/2 cup roasted red peppers
- 1/4 cup walnuts
- 1 tbsp olive oil
- Salt and pepper, to taste

Preparation:

1. Blend red peppers, walnuts, and olive oil in a food processor until smooth.
2. Season with salt and pepper and serve with veggies or whole-grain crackers.

Time to Prepare: 5 minutes

Servings: 2

Nutritional Value per Serving:

- Calories: 120
- Protein: 3g
- Fiber: 2g
- Healthy Fats: 10g

Sliced Pears with Blue Cheese

Ingredients:

- 1 pear, sliced
- 1 tbsp crumbled blue cheese

Preparation:

1. Arrange pear slices on a plate and sprinkle with blue cheese.
2. Serve as a refreshing and flavorful snack.

Time to Prepare: 2 minutes

Servings: 1

Nutritional Value per Serving:

- Calories: 90
- Protein: 2g

- Fiber: 3g
- Healthy Fats: 4g

Mediterranean Bruschetta with Olives and Feta

Ingredients:

- 1 slice whole-grain bread, toasted
- 1 tbsp chopped olives
- 1 tbsp crumbled feta cheese
- Fresh basil, for garnish

Preparation:

1. Spread olives on toasted bread and sprinkle with feta.
2. Garnish with fresh basil.

Time to Prepare: 5 minutes

Servings: 1

Nutritional Value per Serving:

- Calories: 120

- Protein: 4g
- Fiber: 2g
- Healthy Fats: 7g

Stuffed Bell Pepper Rings with Hummus

Ingredients:
- 1 bell pepper, cut into rings
- 1/4 cup hummus

Preparation:
1. Fill each bell pepper ring with a spoonful of hummus.
2. Serve as a colorful and crunchy snack.

Time to Prepare: 3 minutes

Servings: 2

Nutritional Value per Serving:
- Calories: 90
- Protein: 3g
- Fiber: 2g
- Healthy Fats: 4g

Baked Cauliflower Bites with Lemon and Garlic

Ingredients:
- 1 cup cauliflower florets
- 1 tbsp olive oil
- 1/2 lemon, juiced
- 1 clove garlic, minced
- Salt and pepper, to taste

Preparation:
1. Preheat oven to 400°F (200°C).
2. Toss cauliflower with olive oil, lemon juice, garlic, salt, and pepper.

3. Spread on a baking sheet and bake for 20 minutes until golden.

Time to Prepare: 20 minutes

Servings: 2

Nutritional Value per Serving:
- Calories: 70
- Protein: 2g
- Fiber: 3g
- Healthy Fats: 5g

Figs with Goat Cheese and Walnuts

Ingredients:
- 4 fresh figs, halved
- 2 tbsp goat cheese
- 2 tbsp chopped walnuts

Preparation:
1. Spread a small amount of goat cheese on each fig half.
2. Sprinkle with walnuts and serve.

Time to Prepare: 5 minutes

Servings: 2

Nutritional Value per Serving:
- Calories: 100
- Protein: 3g
- Fiber: 2g
- Healthy Fats: 5g

Avocado Deviled Eggs

Ingredients:
- 2 hard-boiled eggs, halved
- 1/4 avocado
- Salt and pepper, to taste

Preparation:

1. Scoop out egg yolks and mash with avocado.
2. Spoon mixture back into egg whites and season with salt and pepper.

Time to Prepare: 5 minutes

Servings: 2

Nutritional Value per Serving:

- Calories: 80
- Protein: 5g
- Fiber: 1g
- Healthy Fats: 6g

Roasted Beet and Yogurt Dip

Ingredients:

- 1 small roasted beet, peeled and chopped
- 1/4 cup Greek yogurt
- Salt and pepper, to taste

Preparation:

1. Blend beet and Greek yogurt until smooth.
2. Season with salt and pepper and serve with veggies.

Time to Prepare: 5 minutes

Servings: 2

Nutritional Value per Serving:

- Calories: 60
- Protein: 4g
- Fiber: 2g
- Healthy Fats: 1g

Sliced Carrots with Greek Yogurt Ranch Dip

Ingredients:

- 1/2 cup Greek yogurt
- 1/2 tsp dried dill
- 1/2 tsp dried parsley
- Salt and pepper, to taste
- Carrot sticks for dipping

Preparation:

1. In a bowl, mix Greek yogurt, dill, parsley, salt, and pepper.
2. Serve with carrot sticks.

Time to Prepare: 5 minutes

Servings: 2

Nutritional Value per Serving:

- Calories: 70
- Protein: 5g
- Fiber: 2g
- Healthy Fats: 2g

Whole-Grain Crackers with Labneh and Olive Oil

Ingredients:

- 4 whole-grain crackers
- 2 tbsp labneh (strained yogurt)
- 1 tsp olive oil

Preparation:

1. Spread labneh on each cracker and drizzle with olive oil.
2. Serve as a tasty, savory snack.

Time to Prepare: 3 minutes

Servings: 1

Nutritional Value per Serving:

- Calories: 90
- Protein: 4g

- Fiber: 2g
- Healthy Fats: 5g

Cucumber Slices with Olive Tapenade

Ingredients:

- 1 cucumber, sliced
- 2 tbsp olive tapenade

Preparation:

1. Spread a small amount of olive tapenade on each cucumber slice.
2. Serve as a quick, low-calorie snack.

Time to Prepare: 2 minutes

Servings: 1

Nutritional Value per Serving:

- Calories: 60
- Protein: 1g
- Fiber: 1g
- Healthy Fats: 3g

Spinach and Feta Stuffed Mushrooms

Ingredients:

- 6 large mushroom caps
- 1/4 cup fresh spinach, chopped
- 2 tbsp crumbled feta cheese
- 1 tbsp olive oil

Preparation:

1. Preheat oven to 375°F (190°C).
2. In a bowl, mix spinach, feta, and olive oil.
3. Stuff each mushroom cap with the mixture.
4. Bake for 15 minutes until mushrooms are tender.

Time to Prepare: 15 minutes

Servings: 2

Nutritional Value per Serving:
- Calories: 80
- Protein: 3g
- Fiber: 1g
- Healthy Fats: 5g

Melon and Prosciutto Skewers

Ingredients:
- 1/2 cup melon, cubed
- 2 slices prosciutto, cut into small pieces
- Fresh mint leaves for garnish

Preparation:
1. Thread melon cubes and prosciutto onto skewers.
2. Garnish with fresh mint leaves and serve.

Time to Prepare: 5 minutes

Servings: 2

Nutritional Value per Serving:
- Calories: 70
- Protein: 3g
- Fiber: 1g
- Healthy Fats: 2g

These snacks are designed to provide steady energy and satiety between meals. With a focus on fiber, protein, and heart-healthy fats, each recipe supports stable blood sugar levels and digestive health while satisfying cravings in a health-conscious way.

Preview of Chapter 7: Simple and Satisfying Mediterranean Desserts

In Chapter 7, we'll dive into wholesome Mediterranean-inspired desserts that are both satisfying and nourishing. These desserts focus on natural sweetness from fruits, nuts, and honey, offering guilt-free treats that cater to seniors' tastes without compromising their health goals.

SATISFYING DESSERTS WITH NATURAL SWEETNESS

The Mediterranean diet's approach to dessert centers around simplicity, natural sweetness, and moderation. By using ingredients like fresh fruits, nuts, yogurt, and honey, these desserts offer satisfying flavors and nutritional benefits. This approach allows for the enjoyment of sweet treats in a way that aligns with balanced eating and respects natural flavors.

Key Components of Mediterranean Desserts

- **Natural Sweeteners**: Honey, dates, and fruit provide sweetness without the need for refined sugar.

- **Nutrient-Dense Ingredients**: Nuts, seeds, yogurt, and fruits provide fiber, antioxidants, and healthy fats.

- **Moderation**: Portion sizes are smaller, focusing on quality ingredients to satisfy cravings without overindulgence.

Recipes (30 Naturally Sweetened Desserts)

Below are 30 Mediterranean-inspired dessert recipes that utilize natural sweetness and nutrient-dense ingredients. Each recipe includes ingredients, detailed steps, preparation time, servings, and nutritional information per serving.

Baked Apples with Cinnamon and Walnuts

Ingredients:

- 2 apples, cored
- 1/4 cup walnuts, chopped
- 1 tsp cinnamon
- 1 tbsp honey

Preparation:

1. Preheat oven to 375°F (190°C).
2. Place apples in a baking dish and fill with walnuts and cinnamon.
3. Drizzle with honey and bake for 20-25 minutes until tender.

Time to Prepare: 25 minutes

Servings: 2

Nutritional Value per Serving:
- Calories: 150
- Fiber: 4g
- Natural Sugars: 12g
- Healthy Fats: 5g

Greek Yogurt with Honey and Pomegranate Seeds

Ingredients:
- 1/2 cup Greek yogurt
- 1 tbsp honey
- 2 tbsp pomegranate seeds

Preparation:
1. Place Greek yogurt in a bowl.
2. Drizzle with honey and sprinkle with pomegranate seeds.

Time to Prepare: 2 minutes

Servings: 1

Nutritional Value per Serving:
- Calories: 120
- Protein: 8g
- Natural Sugars: 8g
- Healthy Fats: 2g

Olive Oil and Lemon Cake

Ingredients:
- 1 cup almond flour
- 1/4 cup olive oil
- 1/4 cup honey
- Zest and juice of 1 lemon

- 1/2 tsp baking powder

Preparation:

1. Preheat oven to 350°F (175°C).
2. In a bowl, combine almond flour, olive oil, honey, lemon zest, lemon juice, and baking powder.
3. Pour into a small cake pan and bake for 20-25 minutes.

Time to Prepare: 30 minutes

Servings: 6

Nutritional Value per Serving:

- Calories: 180
- Protein: 3g
- Natural Sugars: 5g
- Healthy Fats: 10g

Fresh Fig and Almond Tart

Ingredients:

- 1/2 cup almond flour
- 1 tbsp honey
- 1 tbsp butter, melted
- 4 fresh figs, sliced

Preparation:

1. Preheat oven to 350°F (175°C).
2. In a bowl, mix almond flour, honey, and melted butter to form a crust.
3. Press the mixture into a small tart pan and arrange fig slices on top.
4. Bake for 10-12 minutes.

Time to Prepare: 15 minutes

Servings: 4

Nutritional Value per Serving:

- Calories: 130
- Fiber: 2g

- Natural Sugars: 6g
- Healthy Fats: 7g

Poached Pears in Red Wine

Ingredients:

- 2 pears, peeled and halved
- 1 cup red wine
- 1 cinnamon stick
- 1 tbsp honey

Preparation:

1. In a pot, combine red wine, cinnamon stick, and honey. Bring to a simmer.
2. Add pear halves and poach for 10-15 minutes until tender.
3. Serve warm or chilled.

Time to Prepare: 20 minutes

Servings: 2

Nutritional Value per Serving:

- Calories: 110
- Fiber: 3g
- Natural Sugars: 9g
- Antioxidants: High

Ricotta with Fresh Strawberries and Honey

Ingredients:

- 1/4 cup ricotta cheese
- 1/4 cup fresh strawberries, sliced
- 1 tsp honey

Preparation:

1. Place ricotta in a bowl and top with strawberries.
2. Drizzle with honey and serve.

Time to Prepare: 2 minutes

Servings: 1

Nutritional Value per Serving:
- Calories: 90
- Protein: 4g
- Natural Sugars: 6g
- Healthy Fats: 3g

Orange and Almond Flourless Cake

Ingredients:
- 1/2 cup almond flour
- 1/4 cup honey
- Zest of 1 orange
- 1/4 cup orange juice

Preparation:
1. Preheat oven to 350°F (175°C).
2. Mix almond flour, honey, orange zest, and juice until well combined.
3. Pour into a small baking dish and bake for 20 minutes.

Time to Prepare: 25 minutes

Servings: 4

Nutritional Value per Serving:
- Calories: 130
- Fiber: 2g
- Natural Sugars: 10g
- Healthy Fats: 6g

Stuffed Dates with Almonds and Coconut

Ingredients:
- 4 Medjool dates, pitted
- 4 almonds

- 1 tbsp shredded coconut

Preparation:

1. Insert one almond into each date.
2. Roll in shredded coconut and serve.

Time to Prepare: 5 minutes

Servings: 2

Nutritional Value per Serving:

- Calories: 70
- Fiber: 2g
- Natural Sugars: 8g
- Healthy Fats: 3g

Lemon Yogurt Parfait with Berries

Ingredients:

- 1/2 cup Greek yogurt
- 1/4 cup mixed berries
- Zest of 1/2 lemon
- 1 tsp honey

Preparation:

1. Layer Greek yogurt and berries in a bowl.
2. Top with lemon zest and drizzle with honey.

Time to Prepare: 5 minutes

Servings: 1

Nutritional Value per Serving:

- Calories: 100
- Protein: 8g
- Fiber: 2g
- Natural Sugars: 8g

Watermelon with Feta and Mint

Ingredients:

- 1/2 cup watermelon cubes
- 1 tbsp crumbled feta cheese
- Fresh mint leaves, chopped

Preparation:

1. In a bowl, combine watermelon, feta, and mint.
2. Serve as a refreshing summer dessert.

Time to Prepare: 3 minutes

Servings: 1

Nutritional Value per Serving:

- Calories: 60
- Protein: 2g
- Fiber: 1g
- Healthy Fats: 2g

Peach and Honey Skillet Crisp

Ingredients:

- 2 peaches, sliced
- 1/4 cup rolled oats
- 1 tbsp almond flour
- 1 tbsp honey
- 1 tbsp coconut oil, melted
- 1/4 tsp cinnamon

Preparation:

1. Preheat oven to 350°F (175°C).
2. In a bowl, toss peaches with honey and cinnamon.
3. In a separate bowl, combine oats, almond flour, and coconut oil.
4. Layer peaches in a small skillet or baking dish and sprinkle the oat mixture on top.
5. Bake for 20-25 minutes until golden and bubbly.

Time to Prepare: 30 minutes

Servings: 2

Nutritional Value per Serving:

- Calories: 160
- Fiber: 3g
- Natural Sugars: 10g
- Healthy Fats: 5g

Frozen Banana Bites with Dark Chocolate

Ingredients:

- 1 banana, sliced
- 2 tbsp dark chocolate chips, melted
- 1 tbsp crushed almonds (optional)

Preparation:

1. Dip each banana slice in melted dark chocolate.

2. Sprinkle with crushed almonds if desired.
3. Place on a baking sheet lined with parchment paper and freeze for 1 hour.

Time to Prepare: 10 minutes (plus 1 hour freezing)

Servings: 2

Nutritional Value per Serving:
- Calories: 120
- Fiber: 3g
- Natural Sugars: 10g
- Healthy Fats: 4g

Oat and Almond Cookies

Ingredients:
- 1/2 cup rolled oats
- 1/4 cup almond flour
- 1 tbsp honey
- 1 tbsp coconut oil, melted
- 1/2 tsp vanilla extract

Preparation:
1. Preheat oven to 350°F (175°C).
2. In a bowl, combine oats, almond flour, honey, coconut oil, and vanilla extract.
3. Scoop spoonfuls onto a baking sheet and flatten slightly.
4. Bake for 10-12 minutes until golden.

Time to Prepare: 15 minutes

Servings: 6 cookies

Nutritional Value per Serving:
- Calories: 70
- Fiber: 1g
- Natural Sugars: 4g
- Healthy Fats: 3g

Lemon Ricotta Cheesecake

Ingredients:

- 1/2 cup ricotta cheese
- 1 tbsp honey
- Zest of 1/2 lemon
- 1/4 tsp vanilla extract

Preparation:

1. Preheat oven to 350°F (175°C).
2. In a bowl, combine ricotta, honey, lemon zest, and vanilla extract.
3. Pour into a small ramekin and bake for 15-20 minutes until set.

Time to Prepare: 20 minutes

Servings: 2

Nutritional Value per Serving:

- Calories: 90
- Protein: 5g
- Natural Sugars: 4g
- Healthy Fats: 4g

Baked Pears with Cinnamon and Almonds

Ingredients:

- 2 pears, halved and cored
- 1 tbsp honey
- 1/4 cup sliced almonds
- 1/2 tsp cinnamon

Preparation:

1. Preheat oven to 375°F (190°C).
2. Place pear halves in a baking dish, drizzle with honey, and sprinkle with cinnamon and almonds.
3. Bake for 20-25 minutes until tender.

Time to Prepare: 25 minutes

Servings: 2

Nutritional Value per Serving:
- Calories: 110
- Fiber: 4g
- Natural Sugars: 10g
- Healthy Fats: 5g

Dark Chocolate and Walnut Bark

Ingredients:
- 1/4 cup dark chocolate chips, melted
- 2 tbsp chopped walnuts

Preparation:
1. Spread melted chocolate onto a parchment-lined baking sheet.
2. Sprinkle chopped walnuts over the chocolate.
3. Refrigerate until firm, then break into pieces.

Time to Prepare: 10 minutes (plus cooling)

Servings: 2

Nutritional Value per Serving:
- Calories: 100
- Fiber: 2g
- Natural Sugars: 5g
- Healthy Fats: 6g

Berry and Almond Crumble

Ingredients:
- 1/2 cup mixed berries
- 2 tbsp almond flour
- 1 tbsp oats
- 1 tbsp honey

- 1/2 tbsp coconut oil, melted

Preparation:

1. Preheat oven to 350°F (175°C).
2. In a small baking dish, layer berries and drizzle with honey.
3. Combine almond flour, oats, and coconut oil, then sprinkle over berries.
4. Bake for 15-20 minutes.

Time to Prepare: 20 minutes

Servings: 2

Nutritional Value per Serving:

- Calories: 130
- Fiber: 3g
- Natural Sugars: 8g
- Healthy Fats: 5g

Sliced Oranges with Pistachios and Honey

Ingredients:

- 1 orange, sliced
- 1 tbsp chopped pistachios
- 1 tsp honey

Preparation:

1. Arrange orange slices on a plate.
2. Sprinkle with pistachios and drizzle with honey.

Time to Prepare: 2 minutes

Servings: 1

Nutritional Value per Serving:

- Calories: 90
- Fiber: 2g
- Natural Sugars: 10g
- Healthy Fats: 3g

Greek-Style Rice Pudding

Ingredients:

- 1/2 cup cooked rice
- 1/4 cup almond milk
- 1 tsp honey
- Cinnamon, for sprinkling

Preparation:

1. In a pot, heat rice and almond milk over medium heat.
2. Stir in honey and sprinkle with cinnamon.

Time to Prepare: 10 minutes

Servings: 1

Nutritional Value per Serving:

- Calories: 100
- Fiber: 1g
- Natural Sugars: 4g
- Healthy Fats: 2g

Coconut Yogurt with Mango and Lime

Ingredients:
- 1/2 cup coconut yogurt
- 1/4 cup diced mango
- Zest of 1/2 lime

Preparation:
1. Place coconut yogurt in a bowl.
2. Top with mango and lime zest.

Time to Prepare: 2 minutes

Servings: 1

Nutritional Value per Serving:
- Calories: 110
- Fiber: 2g
- Natural Sugars: 8g
- Healthy Fats: 4g

Baked Figs with Honey and Almonds

Ingredients:
- 4 fresh figs, halved
- 1 tbsp honey
- 1 tbsp chopped almonds

Preparation:
1. Preheat oven to 350°F (175°C).
2. Place figs on a baking sheet, drizzle with honey, and sprinkle with almonds.
3. Bake for 10 minutes.

Time to Prepare: 15 minutes

Servings: 2

Nutritional Value per Serving:
- Calories: 90
- Fiber: 2g
- Natural Sugars: 8g

- Healthy Fats: 3g

Fresh Melon with Prosciutto

Ingredients:

- 1/2 cup melon, cubed
- 2 slices prosciutto

Preparation:

1. Wrap prosciutto around melon cubes.
2. Serve as a refreshing, savory-sweet treat.

Time to Prepare: 2 minutes

Servings: 1

Nutritional Value per Serving:

- Calories: 70
- Fiber: 1g
- Natural Sugars: 5g
- Protein: 4g

Apple and Date Bars

Ingredients:

- 1/2 cup oats
- 1/4 cup dates, pitted and chopped
- 1/4 cup applesauce
- 1 tbsp almond butter

Preparation:

1. Preheat oven to 350°F (175°C).
2. In a bowl, mix oats, dates, applesauce, and almond butter.
3. Press into a small baking dish and bake for 15-20 minutes.

Time to Prepare: 20 minutes

Servings: 4 bars

Nutritional Value per Serving:

- Calories: 90
- Fiber: 2g
- Natural Sugars: 6g
- Healthy Fats: 2g

Raspberry Sorbet with Basil

Ingredients:

- 1 cup frozen raspberries
- 1 tbsp honey
- Fresh basil, for garnish

Preparation:

1. In a blender, combine frozen raspberries and honey until smooth.
2. Garnish with basil and serve immediately.

Time to Prepare: 5 minutes

Servings: 2

Nutritional Value per Serving:

- Calories: 60
- Fiber: 4g
- Natural Sugars: 6g
- Antioxidants: High

Tahini and Dark Chocolate Cookies

Ingredients:

- 1/4 cup almond flour
- 1 tbsp tahini
- 1 tbsp honey
- 1 tbsp dark chocolate chips

Preparation:

1. Preheat oven to 350°F (175°C).

2. Mix almond flour, tahini, honey, and chocolate chips.
3. Drop spoonfuls onto a baking sheet and bake for 10-12 minutes.

Time to Prepare: 15 minutes

Servings: 6 cookies

Nutritional Value per Serving:
- Calories: 80
- Fiber: 1g
- Natural Sugars: 3g
- Healthy Fats: 4g

Vanilla Chia Pudding with Berries

Ingredients:
- 1/2 cup almond milk
- 1 tbsp chia seeds
- 1/2 tsp vanilla extract
- Mixed berries for topping

Preparation:
1. Combine almond milk, chia seeds, and vanilla. Refrigerate for at least 1 hour.
2. Top with berries before serving.

Time to Prepare: 5 minutes (plus 1 hour chilling)

Servings: 1

Nutritional Value per Serving:
- Calories: 90
- Fiber: 4g
- Natural Sugars: 4g
- Healthy Fats: 3g

Roasted Grapes with Greek Yogurt

Ingredients:
- 1/2 cup red grapes
- 1 tsp olive oil
- 1/2 cup Greek yogurt

Preparation:
1. Preheat oven to 375°F (190°C).
2. Toss grapes with olive oil and roast for 10 minutes.
3. Serve over Greek yogurt.

Time to Prepare: 15 minutes

Servings: 1

Nutritional Value per Serving:
- Calories: 100
- Fiber: 2g
- Natural Sugars: 8g
- Protein: 5g

Lemon and Olive Oil Biscotti

Ingredients:
- 1/2 cup almond flour
- 1 tbsp olive oil
- Zest of 1 lemon
- 1 tbsp honey

Preparation:
1. Preheat oven to 350°F (175°C).
2. Mix almond flour, olive oil, lemon zest, and honey.
3. Shape into logs, bake for 15 minutes, and slice into biscotti.

Time to Prepare: 20 minutes

Servings: 6 biscotti

Nutritional Value per Serving:
- Calories: 80
- Fiber: 1g
- Natural Sugars: 3g
- Healthy Fats: 5g

Fresh Berries with Creamy Ricotta

Ingredients:
- 1/2 cup mixed berries
- 1/4 cup ricotta cheese
- 1 tsp honey

Preparation:
1. Place berries in a bowl and top with ricotta.
2. Drizzle with honey.

Time to Prepare: 2 minutes

Servings: 1

Nutritional Value per Serving:
- Calories: 90
- Fiber: 3g
- Natural Sugars: 7g
- Protein: 4g

Dark Chocolate and Date Truffles

Ingredients:

- 1/2 cup dates, pitted
- 1 tbsp cocoa powder
- 1 tbsp crushed almonds

Preparation:

1. In a food processor, blend dates until smooth.
2. Roll into balls and coat with cocoa powder and crushed almonds.

Time to Prepare: 10 minutes

Servings: 6 truffles

Nutritional Value per Serving:

- Calories: 60
- Fiber: 2g
- Natural Sugars: 6g
- Healthy Fats: 2g

These dessert recipes provide naturally sweetened options that prioritize nutrient-dense ingredients over refined sugars. Each dessert includes beneficial nutrients like fiber, antioxidants, and healthy fats, making them a satisfying and health-conscious choice for seniors.

Preview of Chapter 9: Nourishing Beverages and Smoothies

In Chapter 9, we'll dive into a variety of nourishing beverages and smoothies inspired by the Mediterranean lifestyle. From hydrating teas to nutrient-packed smoothies, these drinks support digestion, hydration, and provide a refreshing way to enjoy essential vitamins and minerals.

MEAL PLANNING FOR SENIORS – MAKING IT EASY AND ENJOYABLE

Aging often brings new priorities and a fresh focus on well-being, but it also comes with unique challenges, especially when it comes to meal preparation. Many seniors find themselves in situations where cooking can feel overwhelming or exhausting, and grocery shopping may become a burdensome task. Yet, as we've explored in the previous chapters, eating nutritious, delicious meals doesn't have to be complicated. With a bit of planning, the Mediterranean way of eating becomes not only achievable but deeply satisfying.

Meal planning offers seniors the gift of convenience, organization, and a sense of empowerment. With a well-thought-out plan, there's no need to worry about what's for dinner or scramble to prepare a last-minute meal. Instead, meal planning allows you to enjoy the benefits of balanced nutrition while saving time and energy. Plus, it can add enjoyment to each week, allowing you to feel more connected to the food you eat and the healthy choices you're making.

In this chapter, we'll cover everything you need to make meal planning easy and enjoyable, including:

- **Sample Meal Plans**: Three diverse 7-day meal plans tailored for different health goals—heart health, inflammation reduction, and sustained energy—will guide you in creating meals that suit your personal needs.

- **Shopping Tips and Essential Pantry Staples**: Stocking a pantry with Mediterranean essentials makes cooking easier and faster, especially on days when energy may be lower.

- **Meal Prep Tips**: Simple steps for preparing ingredients in advance, so you can spend less time in the kitchen and more time enjoying life.
- **Special Dietary Adjustments**: Quick tips for adapting recipes to accommodate low-sodium, low-sugar, and other dietary needs common among seniors.

Meal planning is more than just a strategy for saving time—it's a powerful way to take charge of your health, reduce stress, and create a daily routine that supports your well-being. In the pages that follow, you'll find practical advice and encouraging guidance to help you build a Mediterranean meal plan that aligns with your goals, lifestyle, and tastes, making every meal a nourishing moment. Let's get started on creating a meal plan that brings ease, enjoyment, and health to your everyday life.

Weekly Meal Plan Samples

Here are three 3-day meal plans tailored to specific needs: heart health, inflammation reduction, and energy maintenance. Each includes breakfast, lunch, dinner, and a snack, with Mediterranean-inspired recipes that prioritize health and simplicity.

Sample Meal Plan for Heart Health

This plan incorporates heart-friendly foods rich in fiber, omega-3 fatty acids, and antioxidants to support cardiovascular health.

Day 1

- **Breakfast**: Greek yogurt with walnuts and fresh berries
- **Lunch**: Mixed greens with chickpeas, cucumber, tomatoes, and olive oil dressing
- **Dinner**: Baked salmon with lemon and steamed asparagus
- **Snack**: Apple slices with almond butter

Day 2

- **Breakfast**: Oatmeal with chia seeds, fresh blueberries, and a drizzle of honey
- **Lunch**: Whole-grain wrap with hummus, spinach, and shredded carrots
- **Dinner**: Grilled chicken breast with quinoa and roasted vegetables
- **Snack**: Cucumber slices with Greek yogurt dip

Day 3

- **Breakfast**: Avocado toast on whole-grain bread with cherry tomatoes
- **Lunch**: Lentil salad with diced peppers, parsley, and olive oil

- **Dinner**: Roasted cod with a side of sautéed spinach and garlic
- **Snack**: A handful of mixed nuts

Sample Meal Plan for Inflammation Reduction

This plan includes anti-inflammatory foods like leafy greens, berries, nuts, fatty fish, and spices like turmeric to support joint health and reduce inflammation.

Day 1
- **Breakfast**: Smoothie with spinach, banana, and almond milk
- **Lunch**: Warm Mediterranean grain bowl with quinoa, kale, and avocado
- **Dinner**: Roasted sweet potatoes and chickpeas with turmeric and cumin
- **Snack**: Orange slices with a sprinkle of cinnamon

Day 2
- **Breakfast**: Chia pudding with berries and a drizzle of honey
- **Lunch**: Greek salad with cucumber, olives, and feta cheese
- **Dinner**: Grilled mackerel with steamed broccoli and olive oil
- **Snack**: Dark chocolate square with walnuts

Day 3
- **Breakfast**: Whole-grain toast with almond butter and sliced strawberries
- **Lunch**: Mixed greens with beets, pumpkin seeds, and balsamic vinegar
- **Dinner**: Lentil and spinach soup
- **Snack**: Celery sticks with hummus

Sample Meal Plan for Energy Maintenance

This plan prioritizes complex carbs, lean protein, and healthy fats for steady energy throughout the day.

Day 1
- **Breakfast**: Greek yogurt parfait with oats, almonds, and fresh berries
- **Lunch**: Roasted vegetable bowl with farro and feta

- **Dinner**: Lemon herb shrimp skewers with couscous
- **Snack**: A handful of trail mix with nuts and dried fruit

Day 2
- **Breakfast**: Overnight oats with cinnamon, apples, and a spoonful of almond butter
- **Lunch**: Chickpea salad with tomatoes, cucumbers, and olive oil
- **Dinner**: Chicken souvlaki with roasted bell peppers and a side of tzatziki
- **Snack**: Cottage cheese with pineapple

Day 3
- **Breakfast**: Smoothie with spinach, banana, and peanut butter
- **Lunch**: Lentil and quinoa salad with diced bell peppers and parsley
- **Dinner**: Baked cod with olive tapenade and a side of green beans
- **Snack**: Cucumber slices with cottage cheese

Meal Prep Tips for Efficiency and Enjoyment

Meal prep can make mealtimes less demanding and provide flexibility for seniors who may have varying energy levels or limited mobility.

1. **Batch Cooking**: Prepare large portions of grains, proteins, and roasted vegetables that can be used across multiple meals.
2. **Label and Store**: Portion meals into containers labeled with the date and contents, making it easier to grab what you need without confusion.
3. **Freezer-Friendly Options**: Soups, stews, and casseroles freeze well, allowing for quick, nutritious options on busy days.
4. **Use Multi-Purpose Ingredients**: Choose versatile ingredients like cooked quinoa or roasted chicken that can be added to salads, grain bowls, or wraps.

Recommended Kitchen Tools for Seniors

- **Slow Cooker**: Ideal for preparing one-pot meals like stews, soups, and casseroles.
- **Food Processor**: Helpful for chopping, shredding, and blending, reducing the time and effort needed for meal prep.
- **Ergonomic Utensils**: Invest in tools with larger handles that are easier to grip, making cooking more comfortable.

Planning for Special Dietary Needs

To make meal planning accessible to a range of dietary requirements, here are simple adaptations for common senior dietary needs.

Low-Sodium Adjustments

- Use herbs, spices, and citrus to add flavor without salt.
- Choose low-sodium broths and canned goods or make your own stocks at home.
- Avoid processed foods that tend to be high in sodium.

Low-Sugar Options

- Opt for natural sweeteners like honey, dates, or fresh fruits instead of refined sugar.
- Use unsweetened Greek yogurt as a base for desserts or smoothies.
- Incorporate naturally sweet fruits like berries, apples, and pears for snacks and desserts.

Adjustments for Digestive Health

- Include fiber-rich foods like whole grains, vegetables, and legumes to support digestion.
- Avoid heavy or fried foods, which can be difficult to digest.
- Incorporate probiotic-rich foods like Greek yogurt or kefir to promote gut health.

Essential Shopping List for Mediterranean Meal Planning

A well-stocked pantry can simplify meal planning and ensure you have everything you need for delicious Mediterranean-inspired meals. Here's a basic shopping list to get started:

- **Proteins**: Chicken breast, salmon, canned tuna, Greek yogurt, eggs, legumes (chickpeas, lentils)
- **Whole Grains**: Quinoa, farro, bulgur, brown rice, whole-grain bread or wraps
- **Fresh Produce**: Leafy greens (spinach, kale), bell peppers, tomatoes, zucchini, cucumber, berries, apples, avocados
- **Healthy Fats**: Extra-virgin olive oil, nuts (walnuts, almonds), seeds (chia, flax)
- **Herbs & Spices**: Basil, oregano, rosemary, turmeric, cinnamon, cumin
- **Pantry Essentials**: Canned tomatoes, olives, feta cheese, tahini, honey

This list provides the essentials for a variety of meals and snacks, supporting easy preparation and variety in your meal plan.

Nutritional Highlights

Each of the meal plans and dietary tips above ensures a balance of nutrients essential for senior health:

- **Fiber**: Supports digestion and helps regulate blood sugar levels.
- **Healthy Fats**: Beneficial for heart and brain health, sourced from olive oil, nuts, and fish.
- **Antioxidants**: Found in fruits, vegetables, and whole grains, supporting cellular health and reducing inflammation.
- **Protein**: Supports muscle maintenance and overall energy levels, found in fish, chicken, legumes, and dairy.

Reflection: Making Meal Planning a Joyful Routine

To keep meal planning enjoyable, consider these reflective questions:

- **What are your favorite go-to meals?** Include those in your plan for comfort and familiarity.
- **What meals make you feel your best?** Incorporate foods that energize you and support your wellness goals.
- **How can meal times be social?** Plan occasional meals with friends or family, or set aside time for community dining events.

Embracing meal planning as part of a balanced lifestyle can help seniors feel empowered, stay engaged with healthy eating, and enjoy the journey toward wellness.

Preview of Chapter 10: Maintaining a Lifelong Mediterranean Lifestyle

In the final chapter, we will explore practical tips for embracing the Mediterranean lifestyle long-term. This chapter will discuss social aspects of eating, staying motivated, and finding joy in food and daily routines. With practical insights, Chapter 10 will help seniors maintain their healthy lifestyle for years to come.

30-DAY MEDITERRANEAN MEAL PLAN & TRACKING JOURNAL

This chapter provides a complete 30-day Mediterranean meal plan along with a tracking journal to help seniors stay motivated, monitor progress, and create a sustainable healthy eating routine. The plan offers breakfast, lunch, dinner, and dessert for each day, without repeating any meals, showcasing the variety and richness of the Mediterranean diet. Additionally, a tracking journal encourages reflection on meals, energy levels, mood, and inflammation, promoting ongoing adaptation to personal preferences and health needs.

30-Day Meal Plan

The following meal plan provides balanced nutrition with diverse Mediterranean-inspired flavors. Each day includes breakfast, lunch, dinner, and dessert to maintain variety and ensure meals are enjoyable and nutritious.

Week 1

Day 1

- **Breakfast**: Greek Yogurt Parfait with Berries and Walnuts

- **Lunch**: Mediterranean Chickpea Salad with Lemon-Tahini Dressing
- **Dinner**: Grilled Salmon with Asparagus and Lemon
- **Dessert**: Baked Apples with Cinnamon and Walnuts

Day 2
- **Breakfast**: Whole-Grain Avocado Toast with Cherry Tomatoes
- **Lunch**: Roasted Red Pepper Hummus Wrap
- **Dinner**: Baked Cod with Olive Tapenade and Roasted Vegetables
- **Dessert**: Greek Yogurt with Honey and Pomegranate Seeds

Day 3
- **Breakfast**: Mediterranean Oatmeal with Almonds and Dried Figs
- **Lunch**: Greek Lentil Salad with Feta
- **Dinner**: Lemon Herb Shrimp Skewers with Couscous
- **Dessert**: Olive Oil and Lemon Cake

Day 4
- **Breakfast**: Spinach and Feta Omelette
- **Lunch**: Avocado and Beet Salad
- **Dinner**: Roasted Sweet Potatoes with Chickpeas and Turmeric
- **Dessert**: Fresh Fig and Almond Tart

Day 5
- **Breakfast**: Fresh Fruit and Ricotta Toast
- **Lunch**: Marinated White Bean and Tomato Salad
- **Dinner**: Stuffed Zucchini Boats with Turkey and Vegetables
- **Dessert**: Poached Pears in Red Wine

Day 6
- **Breakfast**: Chia Seed Pudding with Fresh Berries
- **Lunch**: Barley Salad with Roasted Butternut Squash
- **Dinner**: Grilled Chicken Salad with Spinach and Olives
- **Dessert**: Ricotta with Fresh Strawberries and Honey

Day 7

- **Breakfast**: Shakshuka with Bell Peppers
- **Lunch**: Couscous Salad with Feta and Cucumbers
- **Dinner**: Greek Beef Kofta with Tzatziki and Mixed Greens
- **Dessert**: Orange and Almond Flourless Cake

Week 2

Day 8

- **Breakfast**: Cottage Cheese with Fresh Melon and Mint
- **Lunch**: Kale and Cannellini Bean Salad
- **Dinner**: Spinach and Feta-Stuffed Chicken with Roasted Carrots
- **Dessert**: Stuffed Dates with Almonds and Coconut

Day 9

- **Breakfast**: Breakfast Grain Bowl with Quinoa and Soft-Boiled Egg
- **Lunch**: Mediterranean Cabbage Slaw with Pumpkin Seeds
- **Dinner**: Baked Eggplant Parmesan with Whole-Grain Pasta
- **Dessert**: Lemon Yogurt Parfait with Berries

Day 10

- **Breakfast**: Honey-Roasted Nuts and Fruit
- **Lunch**: Caprese Salad with Balsamic Reduction
- **Dinner**: Chickpea and Spinach Stew
- **Dessert**: Watermelon with Feta and Mint

Day 11

- **Breakfast**: Whole Wheat Pancakes with Fresh Berries
- **Lunch**: Lentil and Spinach Soup
- **Dinner**: Grilled Mackerel with Roasted Vegetables
- **Dessert**: Peach and Honey Skillet Crisp

Day 12

- **Breakfast**: Savory Oatmeal with Olive Oil and Sundried Tomatoes
- **Lunch**: Warm Mediterranean Grain Bowl with Quinoa
- **Dinner**: Stuffed Bell Peppers with Hummus and Vegetables
- **Dessert**: Frozen Banana Bites with Dark Chocolate

Day 13

- **Breakfast**: Baked Eggs with Tomatoes and Basil
- **Lunch**: Smoked Salmon and Arugula Salad
- **Dinner**: Lamb Meatballs with Yogurt Sauce and Sautéed Spinach
- **Dessert**: Oat and Almond Cookies

Day 14

- **Breakfast**: Lox and Avocado Bagel with Whole-Grain Bread
- **Lunch**: Farro and Roasted Vegetable Bowl
- **Dinner**: Grilled Lamb Chops with Rosemary and Roasted Potatoes
- **Dessert**: Lemon Ricotta Cheesecake

Week 3

Day 15

- **Breakfast**: Cottage Cheese and Berry Bowl
- **Lunch**: Panzanella with Cherry Tomatoes and Basil
- **Dinner**: Spaghetti Squash with Marinara and Parmesan
- **Dessert**: Baked Pears with Cinnamon and Almonds

Day 16

- **Breakfast**: Greek Egg and Spinach Scramble
- **Lunch**: Cucumber, Feta, and Olive Salad
- **Dinner**: Roasted Cauliflower and Chickpea Salad
- **Dessert**: Dark Chocolate and Walnut Bark

Day 17

- **Breakfast**: Fruit and Nut Breakfast Bowl

- **Lunch**: Tuna Salad with Olives and Capers
- **Dinner**: Lemon Baked Fish with Steamed Broccoli
- **Dessert**: Berry and Almond Crumble

Day 18

- **Breakfast**: Overnight Oats with Cinnamon and Pear
- **Lunch**: Marinated Artichoke and Spinach Salad
- **Dinner**: Eggplant Moussaka
- **Dessert**: Sliced Oranges with Pistachios and Honey

Day 19

- **Breakfast**: Apple Cinnamon Quinoa Porridge
- **Lunch**: Grilled Vegetable Sandwich with Pesto
- **Dinner**: Chicken Souvlaki with Tabbouleh
- **Dessert**: Greek-Style Rice Pudding

Day 20

- **Breakfast**: Greek Yogurt with Pomegranate and Pistachios
- **Lunch**: Mediterranean Stuffed Pita with Tzatziki and Grilled Veggies
- **Dinner**: Stuffed Grape Leaves with a Side Salad
- **Dessert**: Coconut Yogurt with Mango and Lime

Day 21

- **Breakfast**: Mediterranean Fruit Salad
- **Lunch**: Roasted Beet and Walnut Salad
- **Dinner**: Mushroom and Leek Risotto with Roasted Carrots
- **Dessert**: Baked Figs with Honey and Almonds

Week 4

Day 22

- **Breakfast**: Pita with Labneh and Cucumbers
- **Lunch**: Cucumber Rounds with Smoked Salmon

- **Dinner**: Mediterranean-Style Stuffed Peppers
- **Dessert**: Fresh Melon with Prosciutto

Day 23

- **Breakfast**: Smoothie with Kale, Banana, and Almond Milk
- **Lunch**: Almond and Fig Energy Bites with Fresh Strawberries
- **Dinner**: Grilled Chicken with Farro and Roasted Red Peppers
- **Dessert**: Apple and Date Bars

Day 24

- **Breakfast**: Banana Walnut Overnight Oats
- **Lunch**: Greek Chickpea Salad
- **Dinner**: Lentil and Vegetable Stew with Roasted Garlic
- **Dessert**: Raspberry Sorbet with Basil

Day 25

- **Breakfast**: Breakfast Bruschetta with Ricotta and Tomatoes
- **Lunch**: Spinach and Mushroom Stuffed Mushrooms
- **Dinner**: Poached Cod with Saffron and Sautéed Zucchini
- **Dessert**: Tahini and Dark Chocolate Cookies

Day 26

- **Breakfast**: Egg Muffins with Spinach and Mushrooms
- **Lunch**: Fennel and Citrus Salad
- **Dinner**: Greek-Style Baked Fish with Tomato and Olive Salsa
- **Dessert**: Vanilla Chia Pudding with Berries

Day 27

- **Breakfast**: Tomato and Feta Stuffed Avocado
- **Lunch**: Tuna and Cannellini Bean Salad
- **Dinner**: Roasted Cauliflower Bites with Lemon and Garlic
- **Dessert**: Roasted Grapes with Greek Yogurt

Day 28

- **Breakfast**: Spiced Apple Yogurt Bowl
- **Lunch**: Warm Cauliflower and Chickpea Salad
- **Dinner**: Baked Ratatouille with Feta
- **Dessert**: Lemon and Olive Oil Biscotti

Day 29

- **Breakfast**: Muesli with Fresh Berries and Almonds
- **Lunch**: Bulgur Salad with Fresh Herbs
- **Dinner**: Moroccan Chickpea and Carrot Tagine
- **Dessert**: Fresh Berries with Creamy Ricotta

Day 30

- **Breakfast**: Avocado Deviled Eggs
- **Lunch**: Barley Salad with Grilled Vegetables
- **Dinner**: Artichoke and Spinach Bake with a Side of Quinoa
- **Dessert**: Dark Chocolate and Date Truffles

Tracking Journal

To make the most of this 30-day meal plan, use the following tracking journal to observe the effects of the Mediterranean diet on your health and mood. Tracking your meals and reflections can deepen your understanding of what works best for you.

Daily Journal Pages

Each daily entry includes:

- **Meal Tracking**: Log what you ate for breakfast, lunch, dinner, and dessert.
- **Energy Levels**: Rate your energy on a scale from 1 to 10.
- **Mood**: Note how you feel mentally and emotionally.
- **Inflammation**: Observe any signs of joint pain or inflammation and mark accordingly.
- **Reflection**: Space to jot down anything special about the day, such as meals that made you feel great or foods that didn't agree with you.

Weekly Reflection Pages

Every week, assess your progress with the following prompts:

- **What worked well?** Identify meals and habits that boosted energy, mood, or digestion.
- **Where can I adjust?** Note any foods to modify or eliminate based on how they made you feel.
- **Overall Energy and Wellness**: Reflect on any changes in overall health, including sleep, energy, and mood.

Wrapping Up: Lifelong Wellness with the Mediterranean Lifestyle

The Mediterranean lifestyle isn't just a diet—it's a joyful, balanced approach to living well. The principles of the Mediterranean way—nutritious food, active movement, social connections, and mindful eating—provide a path to lifelong wellness.

As you continue on this journey, remember:

- **Enjoy Food as Nourishment and Connection**: Savor each meal as an experience, and where possible, share it with others.
- **Listen to Your Body**: Use the insights from your tracking journal to adapt the diet to your unique needs.
- **Celebrate Small Changes**: Each step toward a healthier lifestyle counts. Celebrate every new recipe, every shared meal, and every day you feel good in your body.

By embracing the Mediterranean diet and lifestyle, you're nurturing your health, supporting a vibrant life, and finding joy in the everyday moments of eating, sharing, and moving. Here's to a life full of flavor, vitality, and connection!

Made in the USA
Columbia, SC
01 March 2025

54337096R00087